Statistics for Criminal Justice Using Excel

Statistics for Criminal Justice Using Excel
An Introduction

Allen Lowery

Patricia Lowery

CAROLINA ACADEMIC PRESS

Durham, North Carolina

Microsoft Excel® is a registered trademark of the Microsoft group of companies. *Statistics for Criminal Justice Using Excel* is an independent publication and is not affiliated with, nor has it been authorized, sponsored, or otherwise approved by Microsoft Corporation.

Library of Congress Cataloging-in-Publication Data

Lowery, Allen.
  Statistics for criminal justice using Excel : an introduction / Allen Lowery and Patricia Francis Lowery.
    pages cm
  Includes bibliographical references and index.
  ISBN 978-1-61163-387-0 (alk. paper)
  1. Criminal statistics--Data processing. 2. Criminal justice, Administration of--Statistical methods. 3. Microsoft Excel (Computer file) I. Lowery, Patricia Francis. II. Title.

HV7415.L69 2013
364.0285'554--dc23

                    2013011068

CAROLINA ACADEMIC PRESS
700 Kent Street
Durham, North Carolina 27701
Telephone (919) 489-7486
Fax (919) 493-5668
www.cap-press.com

Printed in the United States of America

Contents

*Note: All chapter exercises are collected at the end of the book
(as opposed to the end of each chapter).*

Introduction

Most people, to include those who are professionals in the field of criminal justice, have a rather large misgiving, perhaps even a fear, of statistics. Often, this fear is seated in a course that was taken years ago, either in high school or while working on an undergraduate (and in some cases a graduate) degree. Very knowledgeable men and women who are teaching statistical courses at colleges and universities make assumptions as to the level of understanding held by the students entering their classes. Often, these assumptions are wrong.

According to many students and colleagues, the stories about statistics courses are the same over the years. Students have passed statistical classes by parroting techniques, but did not really understand. Students ask in-class questions concerning statistical problems, only to be told, "Oh, you should know that." Too often, students have gone to the office of the professor only to leave more confused than they were when they went in.

Students do have a responsibility to prepare themselves and spend an appropriate amount of time studying and practicing. However, fear of the subject matter, and a certain lack of understanding, may combine to cause the student to approach a course in statistical analysis with a certain amount of dread.

Controlling the fear of statistics depends upon two things. First, the student must realize that if he or she can add, subtract, multiply, and divide, they already possess the basic skills necessary to perform statistical calculations. Secondly, the student must take the time to learn the terminology and how to read the statistical formulas. Once this has been accomplished, the mystery of statistical analysis unravels and the sense of dread is replaced with a feeling of satisfaction and accomplishment.

This text has been specifically written with criminal justice professionals and the practical application of statistical processes to criminal justice needs in mind. All examples and exercises have been designed with a criminal justice flavor. The statistical processes reviewed in this text are those most likely to be applied by those working in the criminal justice field. Higher, more complicated techniques are not as likely to be undertaken by most criminal justice professionals in their normal course of duty and have been reserved for later texts.

Statistics for Criminal Justice Using Excel

Chapter One

The Basics: Inferential and Descriptive Statistics

Statistics may be *descriptive* or *inferential*. If the statistics we are using describe something, they are considered to be descriptive in nature. When we are describing something, we will often talk about the center of the data (the *mean or the median*)—just how spread out that data may be and how one point in the data may relate to other points in the same data set. On the other hand, if we are going to infer something (make a prediction) from the data before us, we use the term *inferential*. In other words, inferential statistics permit us to take a small sample of a population and make a prediction (with a given amount of error) as to the statistical parameters (characteristics) of the general population associated with our sample.

As an example, if we had a fairly large group of college students, say 2,000 students total (if we are referring to all of something, we call it the *population*), we may select 200 of those students at random (the 200 students would be a *sample* of the *population*). After collecting information (which may be referred to as *data*) from those 200 students we could make inferences (draw conclusions) about the entire body of students. Of course, since these conclusions would be restricted to the same areas of information that we gathered from our sample of 200 students, the conclusions would only apply to the remaining 1,800 students. Additionally, we would have to deal with a certain amount of error in the conclusions.

Simply stated, we could not make a prediction as to test scores in the first place, without gathering that test score information from our sample. Also, we could not properly apply our conclusions to an entirely new group of 2,000 students. We can only apply our conclusions to the original group from which the sample we used for the test was drawn.

As we are working with statistics, we will use terms such as *data* and *variables*. *Data* is plural, which means we are working with more than one bit of information. If we were only looking at only one bit of information we would use the term *datum*. A *variable* is something (a characteristic) that changes or varies for the something that we are examining in order to collect information on it.

As an example, let's go back to our students. A *characteristic* would be the height of the students. This *characteristic* is a variable because it varies, more or less, from student to student (not all of our students are exactly 6 feet tall).

Variables are classified as either *discrete* or *continuous*. A *discrete* variable will have a very definite and final *(finite)* number of values. As an example, if we were counting the number of students in a statistics class we would have a very definite number, say 35 students. We would not report to the academic vice-president that we have 35.5 students in the class (even though, as all course facilitators have experienced, it is probable that mental absence from a statistics class, due to a substantial amount of daydreaming, might support the reporting of fractions in attendance)!

A *continuous* variable, on the other hand, may have an unlimited *(infinite)* number of values. As an example, if we were to keep track of the number of hours a student actually spent studying for a stats exam we might come up with a number like 27 hours, 14 minutes and 29 seconds. In other words, since the result of our study would produce more than just one flat answer in terms of whole hours, the answer would go beyond a straight hour and break that time down into smaller (and perhaps even smaller) increments.

Levels of Measurement

Variables are also classified as to the amount of information they provide for us. When we describe variables this way, we use the terms *nominal, ordinal, interval,* and *ratio*.

The level described as *nominal* is the most basic. *Nominal* variables allow us to separate one person, place, or thing from another. As an example, if we were to look at the vehicles in a corporate fleet we could say that the fleet is made up of Fords, Chevrolets, and Dodges. This does not give us a great deal of information, but it does allow us to break the fleet down into the make of vehicles. *Nominal* variables do not have a level of measurement, and as such are sometimes referred to as *qualitative variables*. They simply allow us to "qualify" or describe something.

Because nominal variables are only the names of something (they can be organized into a *nominal scale*) we really cannot add, subtract, multiply or divide them in a meaningful way. We can, however, count them. As an example, we could say that we have 27 Fords, 19 Chevrolets and 9 Dodges in our fleet of vehicles. Additionally, we could convert these numbers into percentages. In our example we have a total of 55 vehicles. We could report that our fleet was composed of 49% Fords, 35% Chevrolets, and 16% Dodges. To find the percentage you simply divide the number of a certain make of vehicle, say Fords (27), by the total number of vehicles in the fleet (55) and get 0.49, or 49%.

Just above the *nominal scale* in the level of power of measurement is the *ordinal scale*. Information at the ordinal level allows us to place the data in an order. The ability to set up a meaningful order permits us to compare the amounts (variables at this level are considered *quantitative* variables). It allows us to say that something is better or bigger than something else. However, even with the ability to order the data, we would not be able to say how much better or bigger one ordered group was when compared to another group. As an example, if a person were to respond to a question regarding how satisfied they were with a watch they had just purchased, they might tell us they were either very unsatisfied, unsatisfied, satisfied, or very satisfied. We would know how they felt, but we really would not know how much difference there was in their mind between being satisfied (if they were) and very satisfied. *Ordinal* variables include the power of the level of measurement of nominal variables. In other words, ordinal-level variables include the information found in nominal-level variables.

Third on the scale as we move upward is the level of *interval*. Variables at this level (quantitative) are of greater use than those at the ordinal level, as variables at this level of measurement have equal distances between them. Now, not only can we say that one of whatever it is that we are measuring is more or less than another, we can say how much more or less. An excellent example, used in many stats texts and classes, is that of the Fahrenheit temperature scale. The differences in temperature are in precise measurable units of one degree each. Missing, however, at this level of measurement is an absolute zero. Using the Fahrenheit temperature scale we can record temperatures below zero. With an interval scale we can insert a degree of measurability to the terms of very unsatisfied, unsatisfied, satisfied, and very satisfied by placing a number with the term: very unsatisfied = 1, unsatisfied = 2, satisfied = 3, and very satisfied = 4. While these measurements are not as precise as those in the Fahrenheit temperature scale, they do allow the person answering the question to somewhat assign an equivalent change in their attitude as they move from term to term.

Another interesting aspect at this level of measurement, to return to the temperature example used above, is that a temperature reading of 60 degrees is not twice as hot as a reading of 30 degrees (this is because we do not have an absolute zero and therefore cannot convert our measurements into ratios). Variables at the interval level include the powers of measurement of the nominal and ordinal levels.

The level of measurement of variables that provides the most information, and is inclusive of all of the other levels, is the level of the ratio scale. Variables at this level have equal distances (or measurements) between them, and they have an absolute (or true) zero. No measurement is possible below zero at this level. As an example, you could not report that you have fewer than zero inmates in your jail, or that you had fewer than zero officers on patrol if you were a chief of police.

Many people feel that statistics have to be complicated and confusing if they are going to be useful. In reality, the use of basic statistics, such as the mean, the median, and the mode will prove to be very useful in many situations. This is so because very few of the general public have taken courses in statistics and may be confused by some of the higher-level techniques. Most people will better understand the information you are presenting to them if you present it in terms they are more likely to encounter in the normal course of their lives.

Mean of Population and Sample

The *mean* is simply the average. You find the average by adding up the data and then dividing the total by the number of data points. As an example, if you were the sheriff and interested in knowing the average number of residential burglaries (yearly) that had occurred in your county over the last five years you would add the total of each year's burglaries (53, 42, 61, 49, 38) to get 243 burglaries occurring over the past five years. You would next divide 243 (the total number of burglaries, or X = 243) by the number of years, which is five (N = 5), and get 48.6 burglaries per year. For the sake of clarity we may wish to round the number to an average (or mean) of 49 burglaries per year for the five-year period.

You will notice that a large "N" was used to designate the number of years recorded. Since we are concerned with the average (mean) number of burglaries *per year,* and we were reviewing five years, we divide the total number of burglaries (X = 243) by five years (N = 5). The use of a capital N tells us that we are dealing with a *population.* In other words, we are focusing on all of the burglaries that were reported to our department, during this five-year period.

There is one other point we should make while we are working with the mean. It is possible to estimate a mean when you are using grouped data. Grouped data refers to a specific event that has been collected for a given area. As an example, staying with our law enforcement theme, let's say we have a county that contains twelve villages. In checking our data, we find that three of the villages reported no armed robberies this last year, four villages reported three armed robberies, two of the villages reported five armed robberies, two villages reported experiencing seven armed robberies, and one village reported nine armed robberies. In order to quickly find the mean with grouped data, all we have to do is a little multiplying and then a little division. Multiply the number of villages that have reported a certain number of armed robberies by the number of armed robberies they have reported. As an example, two villages reported five armed robberies, so we would have ten armed robberies. Do this with the data above and you could come up with a total of forty-five armed rob-beries. In all, we had twelve villages reporting, so we divide 45 by 12 and get a mean (average) of 3.75 armed robberies per village. Of course, you can't have a partial armed robbery, so we would report an average of four armed rob-beries per village.

In statistics, formulas tell us when to add, subtract, multiply and divide. The formula to find the *mean* (the average) looks like this: $\mu = \Sigma X / N$. μ (Mu) is the Greek symbol for the mean if we are working with a *population*. A *pop-ulation* would be all of whatever it is that we are concerned with as far as col-lecting data (information). As an example, if we were to ask the same questions of every employee in a bank, and it was only those employees and only this one bank we were concerned with, then those employees would comprise the *population*. While it is nice to be able to work with a population, often is it not possible. We may not know who all is in the population, or we may not have the time or the funds to contact the entire population.

The Σ sign tells us we are going to add (or sum) the numbers. X is the sym-bol that we are using to represent a number, or a series of numbers, that we are concerned with. In the above example of a formula the symbol / tells us that we are going to divide (sometimes this is shown as a straight line under what-ever is going to be divided). Remember, the symbol N represents the total number of data points we are working with. In this case, since we are work-ing with a population the symbol is a capital N.

In other words, our formula is telling us that to find the *mean* of the *pop-ulation* (to use the burglary example above) we should add all of the individ-ual data points (bits of pertinent information shown as X) then divide our total by the number of bits of information that we used. $\mu = 53 + 42 + 61 + 49 + 38$ divided by 5 (which is 48.6 or 49).

Most of the time, however, we will not be working with a population, rather, we will be working with a *sample*. The mean of a *sample* is computed the same way as the mean of a population. We will normally work with samples. Sam-ples are convenient, and can save time and money. They are convenient be-cause you do not have to locate every item or person in a population. This, by itself, can save time and money. However, working with a sample, rather than the whole population, also saves time and money just by limiting the very size of the study required to obtain results. While there is error associated with samples, it can be adjusted for mathematically. Within the *sample* there are the individual points of data, which are called *elements*.

If we are working with a sample we use a couple of different symbols, although the process is the same. The formula for the mean, when working with a sample, uses x with a small bar drawn above it (called "x-bar") that looks like this: $\bar{x}$. Another difference in the formula, when we are working with a sample, is that N becomes "n." When you see these changes you know that the formula is for a sample. Remember, the "x" symbol stays the same whether you are working with a population or a sample, as it represents the individual points of data. If you have several persons, places, or things that you are interested in you may assign a small number to the X so you can tell them apart later. As an example, if you were working with Officers Sam, Mary, Bill, and Fred you might designate them as X_1, X_2, X_3, and X_4. The little number to the right of and below the "X" is called a subscript.

Median

The *median* is right down the center. There is an advantage in using the *median* if you have extreme numbers in your data. The *median* is not affected by extreme numbers the way the *mean* is. The *median* is really easy to find; it might help if you thought of the median strip of a highway when you hear the term.

The first thing you need to do is to put your data in order. Often, the data you receive will be "raw." *Raw* means that the data is not in any particular order. When you put the data in order numerically you are forming an *array*. An *array* may be in either ascending or descending order. As an example, your raw data may be 4, 8, 2, 5, 3, 6, 9, 2, 6, 3, and 4. By placing your data into a descending order you would end up with 9, 8, 6, 6, 5, 4, 4, 3, 3, 2, and 2. Since the *median* is dead center, and we have an odd number of data points, all we need to do is count to the middle, which in this case is the number 4 (there are five data points on either side of the first 4 in the series). If there is an even number of data points, say, 3, 5, 2, 7, 4, 6, 1, 5, you would first form your array: 7, 6, 5, 5, 4, 3, 2, 1. Locating the exact middle causes us to be between two numbers (5 and 4). When this occurs add those two middle numbers together and then divide by two. In our example we have 5 + 4 = 9 / 2 = 4.5, so the *median* is 4.5.

As we previously mentioned, the median is not affected by extreme numbers (called *outliers*), unlike the mean, which is affected by outliers. As an example, let's take the array of 2, 4, 6, 8, 10, 12, 14, 16, 18, 43. The mean for this set of numbers would be 13.3. The median is 11. While this may not seem like that big of a difference, let's suppose you are presenting information to justify a general salary increase for your agency. You have 30 employees who are all making between $20,000 and $30,000, and you have three employees who are making $45,000, and one, your supervisor, who is making $65,000. It is obvious that having extreme numbers, referred to as *outliers*, will cause the mean to be distorted in the direction of the unusually high or low numbers. It is possible to also compute the median from grouped data, but normally you would not be doing this by hand. Your computer will do the work for you and all you will need to know how to do is read the print out, which we will cover a little later in the exercise section of this chapter.

Mode

The *mode* is a number or set of numbers that appear more often in your data than any other number or numbers. It is possible, in some data, that you will not have a mode (there will be no number that appears more often). It is also possible that you may have two numbers, which appear more often than other numbers in the data set, but the same number of times as each other within that data set. As an example, in the set of 2, 4, 6, 8, 9, 10, there is no mode (no number appears more often than any other number). In the set 2, 4, 6, 8, 8, 9, 10, the number 8 appears more often than any other number, so the mode is 8. If we modify the set to 2, 4, 4, 6, 8, 8, 9, 10, we now have two modes (4 and 8). This is because the numbers 4 and 8 appear an equal number of times and that number of times is more often than any other numbers appear. When this occurs we refer to the condition as *bi-modal* (having two modes). While it is possible for some sets of data to be *multi-modal*, the usefulness of the mode as a descriptor is reduced considerably. As with the mean and the median, the mode can be developed from grouped data.

You will have to decide which of the measurements (mean, median, or mode) best describe the data to your audience. Often, all three measurements are presented so that the consumer of the data will have as much information as possible.

One last point on terminology, before we move on to the next chapter, is about populations. As you remember, a population is all persons, places, or things that concern us. As an example, if we were concerned with sworn city police officers in the United States, the population would be all sworn city police officers in the United States. If we are working with a sample, we are looking at some of the sworn city police officers in the United States. If we are concerned with an *element*, we are looking at only one sworn officer. And, if we are concerned with a *census*, we are performing a study of certain characteristics of all of the elements in our chosen population. As an example, in a census we might wish to collect data on the gender, height, weight, race, educational level, hair color, eye color, and age of all of the officers in our study.

Finally, we should keep in mind that a population is what we declare it to be. We could declare that our population is composed of all of the sworn city officers in our own city; it does not have to be all of the officers in the entire country. If we wanted to use a sample, we would then draw our sample only from our population.

Mean, Median, Mode, and More with Excel

While we have been learning how to do some basic calculations using a hand-held calculator, it is also possible to have Excel do the work for us. Using Excel to do our calculations is fairly simple, and may be accomplished in only a few minutes by following a few basic steps:

1. Open the Excel program
2. Click on "File"
3. Click on "Options"
4. Click on "Add-ins"
5. Click on "Analysis ToolPak"
6. Click on "Go"
7. Check the little box in front of "Analysis ToolPak" and "Analysis Tool-Pak VBA"
8. Click on "OK"

Now, when we start to do calculations, and we are at our spreadsheet with the data showing, all we need to do is look to the right (when we are at the "Data" tab in Excel), and we will see a tab on the right side at the top that says "Data Analysis." When we click on this tab, a window will open and from that window we will select the type of analysis we wish to perform. The text will walk you through the steps, and after we do this a couple of times, you will be able to perform the function without any outside help.

As a side comment about the point-and-click ability of Excel, some editions of Excel may differ slightly in the method to be used to set up the point-and-click ability. You may need to explore the program headings and look around a little, but you should be able to figure it out pretty quickly.

First we must enter our data into an Excel spreadsheet.

Officer	Height
1	72
2	75
3	68
4	65
5	70
6	70
7	71
8	69
9	68
10	63
11	77
12	75

As you see, we have one column of data, although we could use as many columns as we want if we are working with more than one data set. In this example we are going to work with height in inches. Once we have our data in our spreadsheet, we will click on the tab that says "Data Analysis." Once we do this, a window will open that is asking us that we want to do.

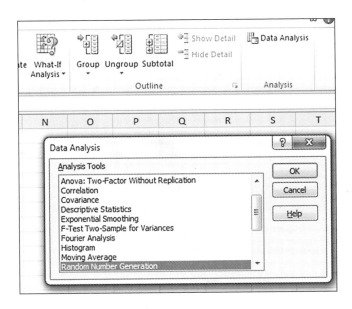

Notice that we have a number of choices to make, but for basic information we will select "Descriptive Statistics." Once you have selected "Descriptive Statistics" and clicked on "OK," another window is going to open that is asking where our data is. While the curser is blinking in the window asking for the data (the Input Range), place your curser at the cell that lists "Height," hold the left mouse button down, and drag down until all of the data is enclosed with a blinking line. Now, release the left mouse button, and you should see where the cell descriptions of where the data is have now appeared in the rectangular window in your Excel spreadsheet.

Please note that the program automatically selects "Columns" for the layout of our data; if we have our data in rows instead, we need to click on "Rows." Also, since we want basic information, we need to click on "Summary Statistics." We need to remember to also click on the little square where it asks about "Labels in First Row." We need to do this because we have labeled the row "Height." If we forget to tell our program that we have inserted a label, it will mess up the calculations, something terrible.

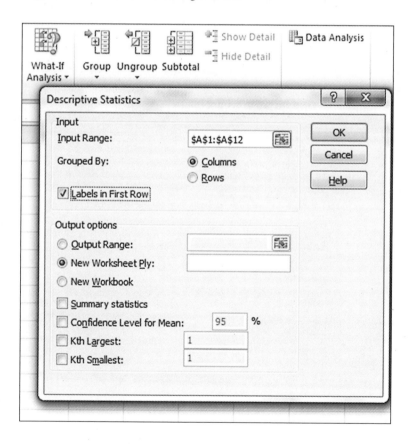

All that remains to do now is to click "OK," and the program will do the work for us. Sometimes the data will show up on a sheet other than Sheet One, but we now have the mean, which is 70.25 in this case (which we would round down to 70, unless of course we want to remain very accurate).

1	Height	
2		
3	Mean	70.25
4	Standard Error	1.187848832
5	Median	70
6	Mode	75
7	Standard Devi	4.114829059
8	Sample Variar	16.93181818
9	Kurtosis	-0.361713917
10	Skewness	-0.035817418
11	Range	14
12	Minimum	63
13	Maximum	77
14	Sum	843
15	Count	12
16		

It is sometimes easier to read the information, if the width of the column is enlarged. While the columns are highlighted in blue at the top of the spreadsheet, click on "Home," then "Format" and then "Column Width." When you do this, the program will ask what width you would like ("12" is a good balance between data readability and conserving space), insert your desired width and click "OK"; at this point the more detailed column information will be more easily visible.

Height	
Mean	70.25
Standard Error	1.187848832
Median	70
Mode	75
Standard Deviation	4.114829059
Sample Variance	16.93181818
Kurtosis	-0.361713917
Skewness	-0.035817418
Range	14
Minimum	63
Maximum	77
Sum	843
Count	12

Chapter Two

Developing Frequency Distributions

When managers find themselves in the position of making presentations to the public, or to others within their organization, they often face the problem have having to make sense out of a large mass of unorganized data. In statistics this mass of unorganized data is referred to as *raw data*. If you want others to better understand the information you are presenting to them, you must organize the raw data in a way that it is clear, concise, and easy to read. A common method of organizing raw data is to develop a *frequency distribution*.

At first glance, the technique of developing the various types of frequency distributions seems complicated. However, like much of what we will be learning in this text, it just looks difficult. In reality, it is really pretty easy, once you understand what is going on. Once we have worked our way through this section on frequency distributions, you will feel comfortable organizing your set of raw data into any of the series of frequency distributions.

Absolute Frequency Distribution

The first and most basic type of a frequency distribution is called an *absolute frequency distribution*. An easy way to think of an absolute frequency distribution is that *it absolutely shows how many times something has happened*. As an example, let's say that the safety director has requested a report on the types of criminal complaints investigated by the police department over the last year. And, let's say that we have organized the complaints into the general categories of physical assaults (without weapons), physical assaults (with a weapon), domestic violence, theft, public disturbance, alcohol/drug, traffic-related, calls for service, and miscellaneous. Going through the actual complaint records we would *absolutely count how many times our officers answered a complaint in each of the categories*. Once we have reviewed all of the answered complaints, assigned them to one of the categories and counted them, we would record the results in a table. Keep in mind that in statistics, when we are talking about how many times something happened, we use the term *frequency*. We may show the frequency in an absolute fashion (just how many times whatever it is we are counting actually occurred) or in a percentage (the number of times the incident occurred, divided by the total number of complaints answered by our department). If we show the data in a percentage format, we call it a *relative frequency distribution*.

To continue with our example from above, let's say that our department answered 342 physical assault complaints (w/o weapon), 27 physical assault complaints (w/ weapon), 56 domestic violence complaints, 654 theft complaints, 78 public disturbance complaints, 123 alcohol/drug complaints, 1,514 traffic-related complaints, 642 calls for service complaints, and 449 miscellaneous complaints (for a total of 3,885 complaints). If we wanted to develop an absolute frequency distribution, using this data, it would look like the example below:

Absolute Frequency Distribution Example

Reported Offense	Absolute Frequency
Assault without Weapon	342
Assault with Weapon	27
Domestic Violence	56
Theft	654
Public Disturbance	78
Alcohol/Drug	123
Traffic	1,514
Calls for Service	642
Miscellaneous	449
Total (N)	3,885

Absolute and Relative Frequency Distribution

If we wanted to provide a little more information, we would continue the development of the distribution and expand the table to an absolute and relative frequency distribution. In an *absolute and relative frequency distribution,* we are supplementing the exact number of times something happened (the absolute portion) with the percentage each category represents of the total crime picture (the relative portion). The N at the bottom of the absolute frequency column represents the total number of complaints answered in the time period under study. We need this number to develop the relative frequency (the percentage column). To develop the percentage, all you need to do is divide the number of times a particular category of complaint was filed, by the total number of complaints (the N). As an example, we recorded 342 physical assaults (w/o weapon) out of a total number of 3,885 complaints. To find the percentage, all you have to do is divide 342 by 3,885 and get 0.0880. To convert this number to a percentage, we move the decimal place two places to the right (8.80) and round to the closest number (9%). Do this with every one of the categories and then add the total of the percentages. You should end up with a total percentage of 100%. (Please notice that if we round our numbers we may actually come up with a total that is a little above or below 100%. To prevent this from happening, which may or may not be important, depending upon what you are doing with the report, keep the number, using at least two decimal points.) If you do not total to 100%, you made a math error or you have a rounding problem as mentioned above. Keep in mind that you do not have to round the percentage to a whole number. You could present the information at 8.8%. Remember, not rounding, or restricting the rounding to one or two decimal places, will increase the accuracy of the information you are presenting to your consumer.

As an example, see the table on the next page of an absolute and relative frequency distribution using the above data:

Absolute & Relative Frequency Distribution Example

Reported Offense	Absolute Frequency	Relative Frequency
Assault without Weapon	342	8.80%
Assault with Weapon	27	0.69%
Domestic Violence	56	1.44%
Theft	654	16.83%
Public Disturbance	78	2.01%
Alcohol/Drug	123	3.17%
Traffic	1,514	38.97%
Calls for Service	642	16.53%
Miscellaneous	449	11.56%
N (Total)	3,885	100.00%

It is possible to continue the expansion of the frequency distribution tables by adding cumulative columns. We do this to keep a running total of the number of complaints recorded to that point in our table, or of the sum of the percentage of complaints to that point. You could even do both by developing an *absolute, relative, cumulative, and cumulative relative frequency distribution.*

Absolute, Relative, and Cumulative Frequency Distribution

First, let's develop an *absolute, relative, and cumulative frequency distribution.* This is relatively simple to do (although it may look complicated at first glance). All we have to add is one more column to the absolute relative table we just completed. As you will notice in the example table below, we have added a cumulative frequency column. This column is simply a running total of the number of complaints answered. The first entry in the cumulative frequency column is the absolute number of physical assault (w/o weapon) complaints answered by our officers (342). The next entry is a combination of the number of physical assault (w/o weapon) complaints (342) and the physical assault (w/ weapon) complaints (27) answered by our officers (369). Continue this technique until you have added in all of the absolute number of complaints. When you are done, the total of the cumulative frequency column should equal the total of the absolute frequency column. If the totals do not match, you have a math error and should go back and check your numbers. For an example, see the absolute, relative, and cumulative example below:

Absolute & Relative Frequency Distribution Example

Reported Offense	Absolute Frequency	Relative Frequency	Cumulative Frequency
Assault without Weapon	342	8.80%	342
Assault with Weapon	27	0.69%	369
Domestic Violence	56	1.44%	425
Theft	654	16.83%	1,079
Public Disturbance	78	2.01%	1,157
Alcohol/Drug	123	3.17%	1,280
Traffic	1,514	38.97%	2,794
Calls for Service	642	16.53%	3,436
Miscellaneous	449	11.56%	3,885
	3,885	100.00%	3,885

Absolute, Relative, Cumulative, and Cumulative Relative Frequency Distribution

The last and most complete frequency distribution table is constructed by adding one more column to the absolute, relative, and cumulative frequency table that we just constructed. The final column is the *cumulative relative frequency column*. You create this column, the same way you created the cumulative frequency column in our last example. Now, however, you are summing the relative frequencies (percentages).

Continuing with the example used in the frequency distribution above, where we constructed the cumulative frequency column, we had 342 physical assault (w/o weapon) complaints, which represent 8.80% of the total number of complaints for the time period. In addition, our officers responded to 27 physical assault complaints (w/ weapon) that is 0.69% of the total number of complaints answered, and so on. As before, the first entry in the cumulative relative frequency column is 8.80%. The next entry is the sum of 8.80% and 0.69%, which is 9.49%. You continue this technique until you have accounted for all of the categories of complaints. When you are done, the total of the cumulative relative frequency column should be 100%. If it is not, you need to go back and check your math. If your math is okay, you will want to take a look at how you rounded (you may have to go out one or two decimal places with your percentages to get the number to come out to 100%). As an example:

Absolute, Relative, Cumulative, and Cumulative Relative Frequency Distribution

Reported Offense	Absolute Frequency	Relative Frequency	Cumulative Frequency	Cumulative Relative
Assault without Weapon	342	8.80%	342	8.80%
Assault with Weapon	27	0.69%	369	9.49%
Domestic Violence	56	1.44%	425	10.93%
Theft	654	16.83%	1,079	27.76%
Public Disturbance	78	2.01%	1,157	29.77%
Alcohol/ Drug	123	3.17%	1,280	32.94%
Traffic	1,514	38.97%	2,794	71.91%
Calls for Service	642	16.53%	3,436	88.44%
Miscellaneous	449	11.56%	3,885	100.00%
N (Total)	3,885	100.00%	3,885	100.00%

Interval Frequency Distributions

It is also possible to develop these tables using interval frequency distribution where the individual data are condensed into intervals. You develop the tables the same way using the intervals that you have created by lumping like portions of your data together. We will be exploring the use of intervals later in this text so we will not develop them at this point. The main thing you have to remember is that the tables are constructed exactly the same way, you simply use the intervals you have developed rather than the categories of complaints. As an example, a table could be constructed showing the height of a freshman class in inches using intervals of five inches (rounding to the closest inch):

Interval Frequency Distribution

Freshman Student Body

Height in Inches, rounded	Absolute Frequency	Relative Frequency	Cumulative Frequency	Cumulative Relative
54–59	113	5.67%	113	5.67%
60–65	473	23.72%	586	29.39%
66–71	782	39.22%	1,368	68.81%
72–77	589	29.54%	1,957	98.15%
78–83	37	1.90%	1,994	100.05%
N (Total, rounded)	1,994	100.00%	1,994	100.00%

There are a couple of points you will want to remember when you construct an *interval frequency distribution*. First, you will want to make sure that when you set up your intervals you do so in such a manner that you include all of your data. Second, you will want to develop your intervals based upon either the size of the interval you want (five inches in the above example), or upon how many intervals you would like to work with (the above example has five intervals). Third, if you decide to use the size of the interval to establish your table it is helpful to remember that people tend to think in certain patterns. As an example, using interval sizes of five or ten usually works well.

If you would rather establish your table using the number of intervals applied to the data, you would have to determine the size of the interval that would work best. To do this, you take the highest number in your data (83 in the above example) and subtract the lowest number in the data (54). Next you would divide the result (83 − 54 = 29) by the number of intervals you think you would like to use. It is generally better not to use too many intervals, say no more than twelve or so. Otherwise, you do not gain much by putting you data into intervals. So, as an example, let's say we want to use six intervals. We would then take 29 (the difference between our highest value and our lowest value) and divide by 6, giving us 4.833. Since we need a whole number, we would round this up to 5. We will have intervals containing 5 so that we will end up with six intervals all together.

A custom that we should follow is to make sure that the lowest value in our bottom interval is evenly divisible by the interval size. In plain language, what this means is that the lowest number in our data is 54, and we should try to divide 54 by the size of our interval, which is 5. 54 / 5 = 10.8. Unfortunately, 10.8 is not an even number, so we have a problem. To solve this problem, we drop one number from the lowest number in our data, which is 54, and make it 53. Now, once again, we divide by the size of the interval we want to use: 53 / 5 = 10.6. Still we have a problem, so we drop another level to 52. We keep doing this until we find a number that is evenly divisible by 5. The number we are looking for will turn out to be 50 (50 / 5 = 10, which is an even number). So our first interval will be 50–54. The second interval will be 55–59, and so on until we have included the highest number in our data. In this example, the highest interval would be 80–84, the interval, which includes the highest number in our data, 83.

Chapter Three

Understanding Variability

When you encounter the term *variability* for the first time, you may begin to feel like you are already lost before you have hardly begun. RELAX, this term simply means the different data points that we are using will vary from each other, as well as from a central point (*the mean*).

In statistics, when you hear the term *variability*, you will also encounter the term *central tendency*. Very simply put, *central tendency* refers to the tendency of our scores to gather around a central point (get it?? ... central tendency). And that central point is the mean of the scores. As an example, if we were to take all of the numerical scores of the students enrolled in a college course on a certain examination and add them together and then divide by the number of students in the class, we would develop the mean (or average) score. If we carefully looked at all of the scores of the class, comparing each of the individual scores to the mean score, we would find that many of them would be fairly close to the mean score. If we look at the number of students with scores greater or lesser than the mean score, we would find fewer and fewer students with scores farther away from the mean. In other words, as we move further away from the mean score, either above it or below it, we would find fewer and fewer of the scores of our students. Most of the student scores would be within one standard deviation (more on standard deviation later, just make mental note of the term). As a matter of fact, approximately 68% of all of the student scores would fall within this one standard deviation of the mean score.

This is a good point for us to stop and learn some more terms and how the calculations associated with the terms work. The terms that we need to be concerned with, at this point, are *range*, *variance*, and *standard deviation*. Once we have mastered these concepts, we will move on to discussing *Z Scores* and the *normal distribution*.

Range

The *range* is fairly easy to understand. It is nothing more than the difference between the highest numerical value in our data and the lowest numerical value. As an example, if the highest number in our data was 100, and the lowest number was 10, the range would be 90. The range is considered to be fairly unsophisticated and is measuring the spread (how spread out our data is), by describing the numerically highest and lowest points in our data. The range is considered to be a measure of variability and could be used as a rough comparison between two groups of data. The group of data with the largest (widest) range would be the group with the most variability between the numbers.

Variance

The *variance* is a more sophisticated measurement than the range. The problem with the variance is that it gives us an answer that is "squared," but more about that in a minute. While the formula to find the variance looks pretty difficult, once you understand what is going on, it is really pretty easy to do. Also, there are formulas that will save you time (short-cut formulas) if you are making these calculations by hand.

First, let's look at the basic formula and talk about what is going on. The formula for the variance looks like this:

$$\sigma^2 = \frac{\sum (X - \mu)^2}{N}$$

Now, let's convert the formula into plain English. The X that you see represents each of the individual points of data (let's use the example of test scores in the college class). Therefore, the X represents each individual student's score on this one test. The formula (the portion above the horizontal line within the parentheses) is telling us to take each individual score and then subtract the mean score of the class from it. Once we have done this, we square the answer (notice the little 2 at the upper right corner of the formula; if we did not square the answer, we would end up with a zero when we are done and we can't do anything with a zero). We do this with the score of every student in the class, then, once we are done, we add all of these "squared scores" together to come up with a total. Now, take that total "squared scores" and divide by the number of students in the class whose scores you were working with (this is the N in the bottom portion of the formula). As an example, let's say the first student was Allen. Allen scored 87 on the exam, and the class mean was 89. Subtract 89 from Allen's score, which gives you $87 - 89 = -2$. Now, square the -2, and you get a squared score of 4. Do this with everyone in the class who took the exam. Add all of the "squared scores" and divide by the total number of students in the class who took the exam, and "presto" you have the variance. See, that really wasn't that hard to do!

Standard Deviation

Now, let's move ahead one more step and learn how to do a *standard deviation*. The standard deviation comes from the variance, which we discussed in the previous section, and converts our data back into the original non-squared units (so it is more useful, than the variance). The term *standard deviation* may be looked upon as another way of saying the "*average deviation*" or "*mean deviation*". In effect, to find the standard deviation, you first find the variance and then take the square root of the variance.... And you have your standard deviation! This may sound complicated, but if you're doing this with a handheld calculator, simply hit the square root key, once you have performed the calculations to find the variance.

This is a good time to introduce a "short-cut" formula. Remember, you can do this on your computer, but, to fully understand what is going on, it is best to learn to work the basics out by hand. The short-cut formula will save you some time if you are working with a larger data set. The formula looks like this:

$$S = \sqrt{\frac{N\Sigma X^2 - (\Sigma X)^2}{N(N-1)}}$$

When we work this formula, we actually find the variance first, and then go to the square root for the standard deviation. In order to work this formula with the least amount of confusion possible, we look to see what we are going to need. First, we can see that we will need to know what N is (the number of students in the class to stay with the example used previously). Then, as we continue to look above the horizontal line first, the formula tells us we need to know the sum (or total) of X^2. To find this, we simply start a new column of data beside our X column (the X column would be a listing of the individual test scores). This new column, the X^2 column, is created by taking each individual test score and squaring it (remember from above Allen's individual score was 87, so his squared score would be 7,569). Now, do this with every one of the individual test scores and then add up (sum) this new column of X^2.

Next, we subtract the squared sum of the X column. How do we know this? Note that the "sum" sign and the X are inside of the parentheses at the upper right portion of the formula, and the little "2" (the sign that tells us to "square" the numbers, i.e., the superscript that is *the exponent*) is on the outside. When you see this, you do what is inside the parentheses first, then you do what is on the outside. In this case, we would add all the in-dividual test scores (remember Allen's original score was 87) and then, once we have added all of the original scores together, we would square that total number. We are now done with our preparation for the top half of the for-mula.

The bottom half of the formula is pretty easy to do. All we need to know is the "N" (remember, this is the total number of students in the class who took the exam) and what "N – 1" is. "N – 1" is simply that, N – 1. This is a math-ematical adjustment to help control error when we are using a sample (this is a formula for a sample, and to be honest, you will be using a sample almost all of the time).

Now that we have prepared, we are ready to work the formula. First take the number of students who took the exam (the N) and multiply that times the sum (or total) of your X^2 column. Next, subtract from this answer the total of your original X column, which you have squared (see the second paragraph above). The next step is to take this newly-derived number and divide it by the total of N times N – 1 (which is the bottom half of the formula). We now have found the variance. All that is remains to be done is to hit the square root key of your calculator and there is the standard deviation! <u>Note: Students often forget this last step, so be sure that you have completed your work and have found the square root.</u>

Standard Deviation Example of Test Scores

Student	Test Score X	Score Squared X^2
Allen	87	7,569
Barb	91	8,281
Paul	85	7,225
Andy	87	7,569
Kari	95	9,025
Alice	98	9,604
Susan	86	7,396
Sally	82	6,724
Robert	90	8,100
Sam	87	7,569
Jim	92	8,464
	980	87,526

N = 11 students

Mean = 980 / 11 = 89

Sum of X that is then squared	960,400
Sum of X^2	87,526

$$S = \sqrt{\frac{11(87,526) - 960,400}{110}}$$

S = 4.657, or 4.66 if we round to two decimal places.

Standard Deviation and Grouped Data

If you look closely at the formula below, you will notice only one difference from our process in finding the standard deviation. The sign "f" now appears. The "f" represents the "frequency," or how many times a certain value appears in our data. When we group the data, we are, in effect, "condensing" several values into a number that represents them more efficiently (from the standpoint of our audience). As an example, if there are five other students in addition to Allen who scored 87 on the examination, there would be a frequency of six (6)—Allen, plus the other five. In order to then condense the class scores to examine how many other students had the same score, the result would be the "frequency" of that particular score.

$$S = \sqrt{\frac{N\Sigma fX^2 - (\Sigma fX)^2}{N(N-1)}}$$

Now, let's work though this. Once again, in order to work this formula with the least amount of confusion possible, we look to see what we are going to need. First, from the formula we know we need a column of X's. In this case, the X's are the test scores, which were achieved by the class on this exam (87 in the case of Allen). The next column is the "f" column. The "f" column is a listing of how many people in the class got that same score (Allen and five others, so the "f" for "87" is 6). The formula also lists a column of "fX." The "fX" column is the "f" (6 in the example above) times the X (87, or the test score). When you see two letters together like "fX," it means that you multiply one by the other. In this case, 6 times 87 gives us a total of 522. The final column that we need to compute, before we can work the formula, is the fX^2 column. Notice that the little "2" (*exponent*) is above and to the right of the X. This means that we are squaring only the X. So, we take each "f" and we multiply it by the corresponding X, which we have squared FIRST. As an example, the score of 87 had a frequency of 6, so we take 6 and multiply it times X^2 (X-squared; $(87 \times 87) = 7,569$) and get 45,414 ($6 \times 7,569$). We do this for each X and its corresponding f, thus creating our final column of fX^2.

Standard Deviation of Test Scores (Grouped Data)

Frequency (f)	Score (X)	X-squared X^2	f times X (fX)	f times X-squared (fX^2)
6	87	7,569	522	45,414
6	91	8,281	546	49,686
7	85	7,225	595	50,575
4	95	9,025	380	36,100
2	98	9,604	196	19,208
6	86	7,396	516	44,376
4	82	6,724	328	26,896
3	90	8,100	270	24,300
2	92	8,464	184	16,928
40			3,537	313,483

N	40
ΣfX^2	313,483
$(\Sigma fX)^2$	12,510,369

$S = 4.308$

Now we are ready to plug our numbers into the formula and come up with our standard deviation. Take the "N" (this is a little different here, so please pay attention), which is the total of the "f" column when you are working with grouped data, and multiply it by the total (or sum) of your fX^2 column. Now, take the sum of your fX column and square it. Once you have squared the sum of the fX column, subtract it from N times fX^2 (which you computed in the first step in this paragraph). You have now completed the top half of the formula.

Take this result and divide it by N times N – 1, and then hit the square root key to get the standard deviation (just like before). Totally confused? Look at the example below that matches what you just did, and it will make sense. It is important to remember that you need to perform a set of calculations many times before you will feel totally comfortable doing it.

$$S = \sqrt{\frac{40(313,483) - (12,510,369)}{1560}}$$

$$S = \sqrt{\frac{28,951}{1560}}$$

$$S = 4.308$$

Z Scores

$$Z = \frac{X - \overline{X}}{S}$$

As you can see from the formula above, finding a Z score is not difficult once you have the mean and the standard deviation. In order to calculate the Z score, you subtract the mean score from the individual score and then divide that answer by the standard deviation.

What are Z scores and how are Z scores used? Z scores, essentially, allow the comparison of oranges to apples. Knowing how to do this, statistically speaking, is very useful. The technique will allow comparisons, such as, the amount of production of individuals across different shifts, as an example.

A Z score tells us where an individual score falls in comparison to the mean score of the data (or group of scores). Let's go back to the example of the examination scores and Allen. We know that Allen scored 87 on the examination, and we now know how to compute the mean score of the class and the standard deviation of the class. To find Allen's Z score, we take Allen's score (87) and subtract the mean class score (89) and then divide the result by the standard deviation of the class (4.66). (See the example of non-grouped data above.)

$$Z = \frac{87 - 89}{4.66}$$
$$Z = -0.429$$

Allen's individual Z score will show us exactly how he did in comparison to the rest of the class, but in order to understand how this works, we need to look at the *standard normal curve* (sometimes called the bell curve). From the above Z score, we know that Allen performed slightly below the class average.

We know this because his Z score is a negative number. A Z score of –0.53 would have performed to an even lower level than Allen, while a Z score of –0.25 would have been a better score. The score of –0.25 is better as it is closer to the mean, even though it is a negative number. After reading about the *standard normal curve*, we will be able to see other uses for Z scores.

The advantage of Z scores to answer questions is more apparent if we use an example, such as, employee performance in a factory across three shifts. If, in the example, a factory, which produces widgets, has a bonus program to reward the two most productive persons. Running one shift per day would make the calculation easy, as the bonus would be earned by the two employees who produce the most widgets during whatever time period is chosen as the bonus period (day, week, month, etc.). However, with three shifts the identification of the two top performers is complicated, by the fact that working conditions and auxiliary duties are not the same on each shift. If Z scores are calculated for the employees of each shift, using the mean and standard deviation for each of the three shifts, the comparison is simplified. See Figure 3.1

Figure 3.1 · Z Score Example of Shifts

	Employee	Production	Shift Mean	SD	Z Score
Day Shift			73.75	3.78	
	Robert	75			0.331
	Allen	78			1.124
	Betty	69			–1.257
	Jim	73			–0.198
Evening Shift			70	4.69	
	Sandra	71			0.213
	William	65			–1.066
	Joan	76			1.279
	Ed	68			–0.426
Night Shift			45.5	3.11	
	Rhonda	42			–1.125
	Rodney	47			0.482
	Marcia	49			1.125
	Steven	44			–0.482

Using Z scores, it is easy to distinguish the two top performers, even when the conditions are different on the three shifts. Joan and Marcia should be rewarded. On the other hand, the worst performer is Betty at a Z score of −1.257. This information would help to support the need for an investigation as to why her production is so much lower than it should be (the next worst producer is Rhonda at −1.125).

Standard Normal Curve

Even though the *standard normal curve* only works perfectly in theory, it is quite useful. We know from our readings about central tendency that the scores of our class on the exam will tend to group about the mean class score. And, as we move away from the mean, both up and down (better grades and people who should have studied a little more), there will be fewer and fewer scores recorded the further away from the mean we get. If we were to graph out the standard normal curve (see below), the class mean would be right in the middle, marked Mu or $\bar{x}$, depending on if we are working with a population or sample respectively. This is the high point of the curve and right around where we would find most of the exam scores. If we would start with the mean score of the class and add and also subtract one standard deviation from the mean, we would find that we would encompass 68% of all of the class scores. As an example, if the mean class score was 80 and the standard deviation was 5, we would find that 68% of all of the exam scores in the class would fall between 75 and 85. If we would go out two standard deviations (plus and minus), or add and subtract 10, which would place us at a score of 70 on the low end and 90 on the high end, we would find that we now are enclosing 95% of the class exam scores. Finally, by extending to three standard deviations, plus and minus from the mean, we would now cover just about all of the exam scores for the class on this particular exam (99.74%) with scores of 65 on the low end and 95 on the high end.

You may have noticed that at three standard deviations we still have not accounted for every exam score. Theoretically, 0.06% of the exams fall beyond three standard deviations. These extreme scores are called "outliers," those exceptional students that ace every exam and pull the curve way up (of course, often class members do not object to the negative outliers in an exam, who tend to help skew the curve in a downward direction for the rest of the class members). Outliers can be found on either the positive or negative side of the curve, or on both sides. As you look at the chart of the standard normal curve, the left side of the centerline (Mu or $\bar{x}$) is the negative side (scoring less than the class mean) and the right side of the centerline is the positive side (scoring more than the class mean). See the chart below.

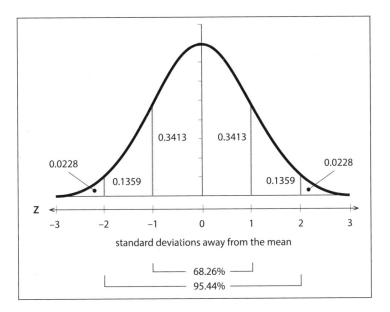

Source: www.wfu.edu/users/palmitar. Retrieved 11/30/2005.

Chapter Four

Comparative Statistics

Crime Rates and the Presentation of Other Similar Data

This section deals with techniques with which you may already be familiar, especially if you are in law enforcement or you read the crime news in the paper. The material is pretty straightforward and should not cause a great deal of difficulty in understanding the necessary computations or presentation of the results in a report format.

The *crime rate* (or any other rate) is normally computed on the number of specific crimes per a 100,000 population. Developing the rate based upon a certain stated population figure allows comparisons between various cities, or other jurisdictions, to be made in such a manner as they make more sense to the consumer of the information. To compute the crime rate per a 100,000 population, you simply take the number of times a certain crime has occurred within a given time frame (usually a year) and then divide the number of crimes by the population of the city (or whatever jurisdictional reference you are using). Once you have divided the number of crimes committed by the population of the selected jurisdiction, you multiply that result by 100,000 to get the crime rate.

While you normally see crime rates per a 100,000 population, it is not necessary to use a per-100,000 rate if another rate would better serve your purpose. For instance, if you wanted to do comparisons between jurisdictions that included areas with smaller populations, it might not make much sense to stay with the 100,000 rate. It might be better for your purpose to use a rate based upon 10,000 or even 1,000 increments of the population. Using a smaller population increment is easy to do; you simply divide the number of times a certain crime occurred by the population of the jurisdiction (just like you did before), but then multiply the result by 10,000 or 1,000 (rather than 100,000) to get the crime rate. You will want to be sure to state in your work that you have used a crime rate per 100,000, 10,000, or 1,000 so your readers will not misunderstand the rate of crime with respect to the population you are working with.

Another point to keep in mind is a consideration of demographics of the various jurisdictions when you make a comparison of crime rates (or whatever rate you are examining). Even if you could compute a crime rate using a population base of 1,000, comparing rates of crime between Chicago, IL, and Findlay, OH, as an example, would not be a good comparison because of the vast differences in the size and makeup of the two communities. Additionally, crime rates are figured on the population recorded as living within the selected jurisdiction. If you are developing a crime rate for a city that undergoes a large influx of workers from surrounding communities, each day the crime-rate-per-population will be inflated, sometimes considerably, by people who live elsewhere but drive into the selected jurisdiction to work (and commit crime).

One last point about crime rates before we move on. There is an easier way to compute the crime rate than multiplying by 100,000, 10,000, or 1,000. Once you have divided the number of specific crimes by the jurisdictional population, you may simply move the decimal point to the right a certain number of spaces, rather than doing the multiplication. For example, to get the rate per 100 population, simply move the decimal point two places to the right, 1,000 three places, 10,000 four places, and 100,000 five places, and so on.

Crime-Specific and Other-Specific Rates

There is another way to compute crime rates, which may give a better picture of what is going on within a certain jurisdiction, computing the crime rate using a more specialized method. As an example, you could develop a rate of late-night pizza shop robberies. In order to do this, you would divide the number of late-night pizza shop robberies occurring within a specific area of the city by the number of pizza shops that are open later at night (in that area of the city only). This method would not use the pizza shop population of the entire city, just the specific area. Then you would either multiply or move your decimal point to the right, depending upon whether you wanted to produce a rate per 100,000, 10,000, 1,000, or 100 pizza shops. This technique would allow the comparisons with similar jurisdictions (by using the same technique in each of the jurisdictions). The result of this specialized method may produce quite different results than figures based upon the entire population.

As a comparison of the two processes: Using a jurisdictional population of 150,000 people and 150 pizza shops open late (past 11:00 p.m.), assuming an experience of 25 robberies at these shops after 11:00 p.m. over the course of a year, a crime rate would be calculated at the rate of 1.67. If the 1.67 rate is rounded up, then the rate would be 2 robberies per year per 10,000 in population. However, if we specialized this analysis and had 25 late night pizza shop robberies per a 150 late-night pizza shop population, we have a rate of 16.66, or 17 robberies per year. The results from the same set of facts can appear to be quite different, depending upon the basis of the calculation and the use of the results.

Using this technique, we could compare the risk to other late night businesses to get a better idea as to where and how we would want to assign our officers. We could also make comparisons to jurisdictions of various sizes by adjusting our multiplier (100 in this example) up or down, depending upon the number of late night pizza shops found in the other city (New York City might have 10,000 pizza shops that stay open late at night). Keep in mind that you can use this technique with any data upon which you need to develop specific rates for some specific purpose.

Percentage of Change

You can also make comparisons of data based upon the percentage of change in the data. This technique is very useful, as it allows for a demonstration and comparison of the change in our data over periods of time. The computation of a percentage of change is not difficult to do.

As an example, let's say that we wanted to compare the percentage of change in reported incidents of alcohol consumption in dorm rooms on a college campus after implementation of an alcohol-awareness program. If the awareness program began at the start of the 2012–2013 academic year, we would want to know how many incidents of in-dorm consumption were reported during the 2011–2012 academic year (let's say there were 243 such incidents). We would then collect data to determine how many of the same incidents were reported during the 2012–2013 academic year (let's say the number now has been reduced to 197 incidents). To find the amount of change (noting that the movement was downward (or negative)), you subtract the number of 2012–2013 incidents from the number of 2011–2012 incidents (243 − 197 = 46). In doing so, we find that there were 46 fewer reported incidents of in-dorm drinking in the 2012–2013 academic year. Next, divide 46 by the number of reported incidents during the 2011–2012 academic year (46 / 243 = 0.189). Now, round

0.189 to 0.19 and then multiply by 100 (move the decimal point two places to the right), and you find that you had a reduction in incidents of 19%. This would seem to tell us that our alcohol awareness program might be working.

It is also possible that the percentage of change may go up. If, as part of our alcohol awareness program, we have an increased enforcement of traffic regulations on campus streets and have specifically targeted driving-while-under-the-influence violations, we may see an increase in this type of citation. As an example, if campus police cited 18 students for driving while under the influence during the 2011–2012 academic year, and with the stepped-up enforcement 27 students during the 2012–2013 academic year, we would compute that we had an increase of 9 citations for this particular offense ($27 - 18 = 9$). We then divide 9 by the original (2011–2012) number of citations (18) to get $9 / 18 = 0.50$. By multiplying 0.50 by one hundred (or moving the decimal place two places to the right), we find that we have had a 50% increase in the number of driving-under-the -influence citations from the 2011–2012 and the 2012–2013 academic years.

Trend Analysis

It is possible that we may want to compare changes in something that we are measuring over time. Comparative statistics provides the techniques we would use to make such a comparison, whether it is over months, years, decades, or any other period of time. As most people tend to understand change better if they can visualize the data, especially if we are going to be comparing data over long periods of time, perhaps many years, we may find it to our advantage to use a graph. Graphs are fairly simple to construct, and most computer programs will do them for you automatically.

As an example, to continue on with the driving-while-under- the-influence data as noted above, let's say that the campus police wish to demonstrate to the campus safety committee the history and current rate of impaired driving on the campus. The officers have researched the police department records and found the total number of driving-while-under-the-influence citations over the last ten years on a year-by-year basis. While they could simply feed this data into a computer and have the computer produce the graph, for the sake of better understanding the process, let's create a graph the old-fashioned way.

Taking a piece of paper, the officer assigned to produce the graph draws a line across the paper from left to right, allowing for margins and perhaps fairly well-centered on the page from top to bottom. Since we are going to be graphing out the passage of years going from left to right (which just makes sense for what we are doing), she then goes to the left end of the line she just drew and draws another line from that point upwards (keep in mind that the length of these lines will vary depending on the size of the sheet of paper and how much data you are going to be recording). She now goes to the left end of the horizontal line (the one that goes across the paper from left to right) and begins to record the years that the data covers, being sure to evenly space the entries along the line. If we are doing ten years worth of data, we would start with 2002 and evenly record the years 2003, 2004, 2005, and so on, along the line until we come to the final academic year, 2011 (which should be at the right end of the horizontal line).

The officer would now begin to work on the vertical line, entering a series of numbers and working up the line toward the top of the page. Since we are interested in issued citations, we may want to run the numbers in a series of "fives" (5, 10, 15, 20, and so on) until we have covered the maximum number of citations issued in any one year during the period of time covered by the study. She may also decide to place small hash marks along the line between the "fives" to indicate the individual citations that were issued.

Now that the skeleton of the graph has been drawn, the officer is ready to begin plotting the data. She would first find the number of citations, which were issued for this particular offense in the year 2002. She would then locate the point that corresponds with the number of issued citations along the vertical line at the left side of her graph. She would then move her pen or pencil to the right until the point of the pencil was directly above 2002. Once she has located the juncture of the number of citations issued and the year 2002, she would make a mark on the graph. She would then do the same thing with the 2003 data and so on, until all of the years and corresponding number of citations had been plotted and marked. Now, by connecting the dots, she is able to create a visual representation of the number of citations issued for this offense over a period of ten years. With a few more minutes' work to label the graph, and perhaps to add color coding, subtitles, or other descriptive information, she has created a very nice looking, professional tool to use in a presentation to the campus safety committee.

Another useful technique, especially if you are presenting data that covers an extended period of time (say 50, 75, or even 100 years or more), is to group the data into intervals. Depending upon how extended the timeframe of your data is, you may wish to use intervals of 5, 10, or even more years. All you have to do is add the data (let's say total citations for driving-while-under-the-influence violations) covered by the years 2002, 2003, 2004, 2005, and 2006 (as 5-year interval), as an example. Now divide that total number of citations by 5 (the number of years in our interval) to get a mean (or average) number of citations issued during each of those five year intervals. Now, go to your newly-created skeleton graph and plot the dot for this interval and the number of citations issued (just like you did before when we were looking at single years).

Now, for one last point on trend analysis and graphs before we move on to a new topic. If you are using data that covers an extended period of time, you may want to consider using a technique known as a *moving average*. Generally speaking, when you do a moving average, you are going to work with no less than five years in any one interval. This is especially true in the criminal justice field as so much can change in the way of influencing factors from just one year to the next. The purpose of this process is to smooth the trend line as it progresses through the intervals.

To develop a moving average in a five-year interval, you first need to develop a mean for the first five years. To go back to our previous example, our officer would add the total number of issued citations for the first five years of the interval and develop a mean. Once this mean has been developed, she will plot it on her graph. Next, she will drop the earliest year (2002) and add a year onto the top end of the interval (2007). Now the interval will be 2003, 2004, 2005, 2006, and 2007 (rather than 2002, 2003, 2004, 2005, and 2006). She will now develop a mean for this new interval and plot it on the graph. She will continue this process until she has covered all of the years in the data. She has now "smoothed" the data with a moving average. All that is left to do is to develop the title and the subtitles for her graph. Of course, as was mentioned at the start of this section, there are programs that will do this for us. In spite of the existence of the programs, it is important to understand the process, as well as being able to explain how the "pretty" graph was developed. It is much more impressive to be able to briefly explain what and how something happened than to have to say "I don't know, I just pushed the button on the computer"!

Chapter Five

Exploring the Relationship Between Nominal Variables

Statistical Relationships

Often you will hear people talking about variables being "related." This means that when there is a change that can be measured in one variable, there is a related measurable change in another variable. As an example, if it rains on a parking lot in the summer, we expect to see puddles form. And, the more that it rains (which can be measured in inches of rainfall), the deeper the puddles will become (the depth of the water in the puddles can also be measured). This allows us to try to explain changes in one of our variables (the depth of the puddle), by what is happening with the other variable (how much rain has fallen during the storm).

It is important to remember, at this point, that a relationship between the variables does not mean that the change in one actually CAUSES the change in the other (a causal relationship). In other words, just because it appears that there is a measurable relationship between the variables, does not automatically mean that one variable is the true cause of the change in the other. As an example, at the moment it began to rain, a water line under the parking lot may have broken and water may also be quickly seeping up through the ground into the puddle. But we will talk more about that later. Just tuck that thought away for now, so it will seem familiar when we bring the topic up again.

Dependent Variable

Here we go, again, with more terminology. A variable may be either *dependent* or *independent*.

The dependent variable is that "something" (*variable*) for which we are trying to develop an explanation for some observed changes or movement in some other "something" (*independent variable*). It might help to think of it as what happens to the *dependent* variable "depends" on what the *independent* variable does. Later on, when we start working with regression and some other techniques, we will refer to the dependent variable as the "Y" variable.

Independent Variable

The independent variable (sometimes called the predictor variable, because we are hoping to use it to "predict" what will happen to the dependent variable) is the variable we are using to try to explain what is happening to the dependent variable. The independent variable is referred to as the "X" variable, and when we have several of them (X's), we number them so we can tell them apart. The numbers are placed just below and just to the right of the X, as an example, X_1.

Contingency Table (2X2)

Now that we understand a dependent and independent variable and have learned some of the terminology, our next issue is examining how to determine whether there is a relationship between our variables or not. The first thing that we need to do is to take our raw data (remember the term from before?) and organize it in such a fashion that we can more easily understand any possible relationships. We will accomplish the organization of the data by constructing a *contingency table*.

A contingency table without the data inserted looks like a bunch of empty boxes stacked up against and on top of each other. An easy way to think of this design is to think of getting ready to play a game of Tic-Tac-Toe. Once you have the grid drawn to start the game, draw another line as a border around the outside of the Tic-Tac-Toe square. The result is one big box with a many little boxes inside.

We call each of these little boxes *cells*. By inserting data into each of the cells as appropriate, we are able to demonstrate what is happening with our data. As an example, let's assume the sheriff ordered a raid of a large party, at which it was suspected a considerable amount of underage drinking was occurring, but the actual significance of the occurrence is an issue. To examine the relationship, the data for the variables is placed in a simple table: a box with four smaller boxes (cells) inside. Across the top, the cells are labeled *male* and *fe-*

male. Drinking and *not drinking* are the labels down the left side of the table. After the raid, the deputies determined that, of the 123 under-aged people at the party (that they were able to apprehend), 72 were male and 51 were female. Of those, 47 of the males tested positive for alcohol consumption, as did 28 of the females. This data would be plugged into the table in the appropriate cell.

In order to examine the data in a usable manner, the sheriff would then add the numbers in the individual cells first across and then down. This would produce a table (see Figure 5.1) that demonstrates that while 47 of the males tested positive for alcohol consumption, 25 did not; 28 of the females tested positive, 23 did not. The marginal numbers (those numbers produced by adding the cells across and down) would tell us that out of all the persons apprehended, 75 had tested positive for consumption and 48 had not (as we add across the table); 72 of the subjects were male and 51 were female as we add down the table.

Figure 5.1

	Males	Females	Total
Drinking	47	28	75
Not Drinking	25	23	48
Total	72	51	123

With the development of the simple table, the sheriff can also produce percentages, which might make the information more meaningful. If the sheriff adds the marginal numbers down and then across, he should develop a total of 123 (the total number of people apprehended); if he does not get this total, he needs to go back and check for a mistake in one of the cells. If the sheriff takes the number of people appearing in cell one (the upper left-hand corner cell—males drinking (47)) and divides by the total of the marginal numbers (123), he will get 0.382 (or 38% of the total number of persons apprehended were males that appeared to have been consuming). If he divides the number in the upper right-hand cell (females drinking), he would find that (28 / 123 = 0.228) 23% of the total number of persons apprehended were females that appeared to have been consuming. Continuing on to the lower left-hand cell (males not drinking), he divides 25 / 123 to find that 0.203 (or 20%) of the total number of persons apprehended were males that did not test positive for consumption. And finally, by looking at the lower right-hand cell (females not drinking), he divides 23 by 123 and discovers that out of the total number of people apprehended, 0.187 (or 19%) of the total persons arrested were females that had not tested positive for consumption. See Figure 5.2.

Figure 5.2

	Males	*Females*	*Total*
Drinking	38%	23%	61%
Not Drinking	20%	19%	39%
Total	58%	42%	100%

It is possible to continue to develop the data contained in this table in various ways. Without going into every possibility, let's explore one more. If we wanted to look *only at the persons who tested positive for consumption,* we would find that out of a total of 75 persons who tested positive for consumption (add the drinking row across to get the total who tested positive for drinking—47 males and 28 females), 47 or 63% were males while 28 or 37% were females. See Figure 5.3.

Figure 5.3

	Males	*Females*	*Total*
Drinking	47	28	75
Percentage	63%	37%	100%

Keep in mind that when you create a contingency table, you generally would place the independent variables across the top of the table and the dependent variables down the side. Not that you couldn't do it the other way, but convention is usually helpful, both to you when you are designing your table and to others as they read it. Also, keep in mind that while the example is a 2X2 table (male and female across the top; drinking or not drinking down the side), you may use more variables and could have a 3X3 or 4X3 or other-sized table, depending upon the number of variables you are working with.

A contingency table will help us (and others) better understand the relationship of the variables to one another. However, we still have not discussed the way to determine just how significant and how strong that relationship might be. In order to move forward in our understanding of statistics, we need to talk about how we measure both, statistical significance and the strength of the relationship. In the process of the discussion, there are a few more terms, which will be introduced.

Hypothesis Testing and Statistical Significance

When we talk about something being significant or something being *statistically significant*, the terms sound similar, but the two terms are not quite the same. In the statistical sense, "significance" refers to an occurrence that is not due simply to chance. In other words, something is influencing what we observe, beyond the possibility the something would occur just on its own without an outside influence. In order to claim this as a statistically significant influence, a method of testing must be developed that would set a standard, or a threshold bar of proof, that we must pass.

The first step in this testing process is to develop an understanding of *hypothesis testing*. Let's say that you have collected your raw data, organized it, and are now prepared to move forward and test your results for statistical significance. While there are a variety of means of testing (which we will discuss and practice later), you must first develop your two hypotheses. While this may seem a little backwards to the way you normally do things, you develop a negative, or *null* hypothesis first. The null hypothesis makes the claim that there is no relationship between the variables. In other words, that variable X (the independent variable) does not statistically exert significant influence on the movement or change of variable Y (the dependent variable). As an example, if we were interested in the question as to whether the gender of a driver is a statistically significant influence on whether or not he or she receives a written citation upon a traffic stop, we could word the null hypothesis as: "The gender of the driver of the vehicle does not influence the issuance of a traffic citation." *Emphasis added: Note that the null hypothesis is always to the negative, or there is no statistically significant change.*

Now that you have developed your null hypothesis, you must develop an *alternative hypothesis* (the alternative hypothesis is sometimes called the *rival* or *research* hypothesis). This second hypothesis claims that a statistically significant relationship does indeed exist between the two variables. To continue our example from above, you would claim: "The gender of the driver of the vehicle does influence the issuance of a traffic citation."

In hypothesis testing, you always run the test against the null (or negative) hypothesis. Once you have run the test, you then make the decision as to whether (and you always use this wording) "to reject" or "fail to reject" the null hypothesis. You never run the test against the alternative hypothesis, and you never state that you accept the alternative or research hypothesis. The reason for this is that you are basing your decision upon this one test. So it is possible that another sample and another test may provide a different result. Also, the presumption is that no statistically significant influence is exerted upon the dependent variable by the predictor variable. If you are a criminal justice professional, it will be easy for you to remember this distinction by thinking of the presumption of innocence found in the due process of law. A person is considered to be innocent (there is no statistically significant influence exerted) until proven guilty by evidence. This may sound like double-talk, but this is the way that it is done, and the process will make more sense once we run a test together.

As an example, you have decided to develop a contingency table (which you already know how to do) to explore the relationship between gender and whether the driver is issued an oral warning, a written warning, or a citation. You place the independent variables of male and female across the top of the table and the dependent variables of oral warning, written warning, and citation down the side. Let's say that your research has discovered that of the 247 women stopped for an apparent traffic violation, 56 were issued an oral warning, 128 were issued a written warning, and 63 were issued a citation for the offense. Of the 321 men that were stopped for an apparent traffic violation, 48 were issued an oral warning, 148 were issued a written warning, and 125 were issued a citation for the offense. See Figure 5.4.

Figure 5.4 · Influence of Gender Upon Citation Decision

	Male	Female	Total
Oral Warning	48	56	104
Written Warning	148	128	276
Citation Issued	125	63	188
Total	321	247	568

Since this table has two gender columns (Male and Female) and three action rows (Oral, Written, Citation), it is referred to as a 2X3 (two by three) table. Notice that we have added the rows across and the columns down to develop our marginal numbers (the totals). Also, notice that when we add the margins down and across we come up with the same total—568. If your marginal numbers do not sum to the same total, you know that you have a math error and need to go back and review your data to this point.

To make our table a little more informative, we may wish to develop percentages to coincide with our basic display of the data. To establish an overall relationship of gender to outcome in a percentage format, all you have to do is divide the number in an individual cell by the total number of subjects in our survey (568). As an example, if we divide the number of males who were given oral warnings (48 / 568), we would find that, out of the total number of drivers stopped, 0.0845 (8.5%) were males who were given oral warnings. This compares to 0.0985 (9.9%) of the total drivers who were female and received oral warnings. Continuing your conversion to percentages for the entire table reveals there may be a slight bias toward leniency when it comes to female drivers. The percentage of female drivers given oral warnings is slightly higher than male drivers (9.9% to 8.5%), but as the outcome changes to written warnings and then finally to citations issued, the balance shifts (only 11.1% of the total drivers cited were female, compared to 22% who were male). It is easy to see, the data makes more sense, once it is converted to a percentage format. See Figure 5.5.

Figure 5.5 · Influence of Gender Upon Citation Decision

	Male	Female	Total
Oral Warning	9%	10%	19%
Written Warning	26%	23%	49%
Citation Issued	22%	11%	33%
Total	57%	44%	100%

Please note: If you add the percentages shown above to the lower right corner, you actually come up with 101%. This is because we rounded our numbers, but if you are giving a presentation, it seems to make more sense to people if you use whole percentages and let the audience know you rounded your numbers, and for clarity, we are showing 100% in the lower right-hand corner.

At this point, it appears there may be a bias involved in the issuing of citations that is linked to gender. However, in order to make a more definitive statement, we need to statistically test our data to see if the differences are large enough to really mean anything (they are not occurring in this sample due to pure chance). In order to do this, we are going to test our null hypothesis: "The gender of the driver of a vehicle does not influence the issuance of a traffic citation." Of course, our research hypothesis would then be: "The gender of the driver does influence the issuance of a traffic citation."

The Chi-Square Test

We can test our null hypothesis by running what is known as a *chi-square test*. While on the surface, this test looks somewhat complicated, it is really very easy to do and simply requires a great deal of repetition as you work with your data. As the best way for you to learn is to actually do, grab a pencil and paper, and let's work our way though a chi-square test using the data above.

Once we have developed our hypothesis, we must learn how to read the formula and perform the calculations to complete our test. At first the formula looks daunting but remember, it is just like baking a cake ... just take it one step-at-a-time and you will get great results.

$$\chi^2 = \sum \frac{(o-e)^2}{e}$$

The first calculation you are going to perform is to compute the expected frequencies. We know from our data what actually occurred in the issuing of oral warnings, written warnings, and citations, but what should have happened if there were no potential outside influences?

To calculate the expected frequency, you follow the directions provided by expected frequency formula:

$$E = \frac{RTxCT}{N}$$

The expected frequency formula tells us to take the row total (the marginal number for the row our subject cell is located in) and multiply it by the column total (the marginal number for the column our subject cell is located in) and then divide that sum by the total number of subjects in the study (the marginal number in the extreme lower right of our marginal category).

Now, let's work this out and see what happens. See Figure 5.6.

Figure 5.6 · Influence of Gender Upon Citation Decision

	Male	Female	Total
Oral Warning	48 (59)	56 (45)	104
Written Warning	148 (133)	128 (120)	276
Citation Issued	125 (106)	63 (82)	188
Total	321	247	568

As an example, looking at cell #1 (numbering left to right and top to bottom), we find that 48 male drivers were issued an oral warning. Looking to the right you will notice that the row total for cell #1 is 104. Going back to cell #1 and looking down, you find that the column total for cell #1 is 321. Multiply 104 by 321 for a sum of 33,384. Now, divide this sum by 568 (the total number of subjects in the study), and you get 58.775. For general clarity (we can't have a part of a person), we will round this to 59. For cell #1, we now know that we would have expected 59 male drivers to receive an oral warning rather than the 48 that did. Write this expected number in cell #1 enclosed in parentheses either below or to the side of the observed number (the actual number of male drivers who received an oral warning).

Now move on to cell #2. In cell #2, our data shows us that 56 female drivers received an oral warning. Looking to the right to the margin, we find 104, and looking down to the margin, we find 247. You now multiply 104 by 247 with the result of 25,688. Divide 25,688 by the total number of subjects (568) to get the expected value of 45.23, or 45 female drivers that we would have expected to receive an oral warning as compared to the 56 that did. Record your expected value (45) in parentheses in this cell. Now continue on to complete calculating the expected value for the remaining cells as shown in the example.

Now that we have found our expected values, let's work the formula for the chi-square.

$$\chi^2 = \sum \frac{(o-e)^2}{e}$$

When we work the chi-square formula, we work it one cell at a time, usually starting with the upper left cell. As you can see from the formula, you take the number you actually observed (48 in this case) and subtract the number you expected (59). Next, you take the result (−11) and square it (multiply it by itself) to get 121. Now you divide 121 by the number you expected (59) for a final result for this cell of 2.05.

$$\frac{(48-59)^2}{59} = \frac{121}{59} = 2.05$$

Record this number (2.05) on a separate line on your paper and move on to the next cell and repeat the process. When you are done (moving left to right), you will have a computed individual cell line that looks like this: 2.05 + 2.69 + 0.41 + 0.53 + 3.41 + 4.40. Sum this line for a *computed chi-square of 13.49.*

Now that we have a computed chi-square, we must compare it to a table (found at the back of this text) to see if our difference is large enough to be statistically significant. In order to do this, we must first compute the degrees of freedom.

Let's stop here for just a minute and discuss what a degree of freedom is. Let's say that we have a string of numbers and that this string of numbers is totaled to produce a sum. For an example, let's use our computed cell line from above. We have six numbers that total to 13.49. All of those six numbers have a freedom to be any number except for one, the last one. In other words, when we add our six numbers, we must arrive at a total of 13.49. Five of the numbers can range anywhere from 0 to 13.49, just as long as the total when we add them together comes out to 13.49. The last number in the string is not free. It is determined by the sum of the other five numbers. If the other five numbers sum to 13.49, the last number <u>must</u> be 0. If the other five numbers sum to 12.5, the last number <u>must</u> be 0.99 in order to arrive at a sum of 13.49. Five of the numbers in the string have freedom, one does not. To find the degrees of freedom in a chi-square problem, the formula tells us to take the number of rows minus one and multiply that number by the number of columns minus one.

$$df = (r - 1) \times (c - 1)$$

In our example concerning traffic citations, we have three rows and two columns, so we would have $3 - 1 = 2$, multiplied by $2 - 1 = 1$, or $2 \times 1 = 2$ degrees of freedom.

Now that we have found the number of degrees of freedom, we consult a chi-square table to find the critical value. By critical value we mean that the chi-square we computed (by adding up the product of the individual cells) <u>must be as large as, or larger</u> than, the chi-square from the table for our test to be *statistically significant.* When we look at our chi-square table, found at the back of this text, we find that, with an alpha of 0.05 (more on this in a minute) and 2 degrees of freedom, our critical value is 5.991.

Before we go on, let's take just a minute and discuss what an *alpha level* is. When we run a test we can choose how difficult we want it to be to be able to declare that our test means something (is statistically significant). Traditionally, an alpha of 0.05 is used (Cohen, 1990), and this is where most computer programs default. When we use an alpha of 0.05, we are saying that 95 times out of 100 something made what we see happening happen ($100 - 5 = 95$; the alpha of 0.05 represents five one-hundredths decimally).

In other words, five times out of 100 what we see occurring is happening just because of pure chance. Or, we could say that if we had a large group of data, and pulled 100 samples out of that same data at random, we could expect to get this same result 95 times. Of course, that means that 5 other times we could get a different result. The problem is we never really know if our current sample is one of the hypothetical 95 that would give us the same result or one of the renegade (if you will allow me to use the term) 5 that would produce a different outcome. That is why we should say something like, "With the data available at the time of the test, our results, at an alpha of 0.05, indicate that … whatever they may indicate."

If we want to make it easier to claim significance, we make the alpha number larger; as an example, 0.10 (90 times out of 100 something is making it happen; 10 times out of 100 pure chance is involved in the outcome). Using a lower alpha number, 0.01, as an example would make it much more difficult to make the claim that our test is significant. This is so because we are now claiming that 99 times out of 100 some outside influence is producing the observed result, and only 1 time out of 100 is pure chance involved.

As an example, with two degrees of freedom and an alpha of 0.01, our critical value from the chi-square table is 9.21. This would be a higher bar for us to cross with our computed chi-square and would give more weight to our test. In our working example above, we have a computed chi-square of 13.49, which is obviously significant even at this much higher (more demanding) alpha level; 13.49 is still as high or higher than the critical value (9.21 at an alpha of 0.01).

Now, let's continue on. Since our computed chi-square of 13.49 is much larger than 5.991, we know that the result of our test is statistically significant at an alpha of 0.05, which is the standard alpha level used in most tests of significance.

When your test proves to be statistically significant you state: "With the data available at the time of the study, and testing at an alpha of 0.05, I reject the null hypothesis." You are *rejecting the null* hypothesis, because your test was statistically significant.

If your test *does not prove to be statistically significant,* you state: "With the data available at the time of the study, and testing at an alpha of 0.05, I fail to reject the null hypothesis."

As you remember, our null hypothesis was: "The gender of the driver of the vehicle *does not* influence the issuance of a traffic citation." The research hypothesis was "The gender of the driver of the vehicle does influence the issuance of a traffic citation."

The result of our chi-square test was significant at an alpha of 0.05 (our calculated value of 13.49 is as large as, or larger than, the table value of 5.991).

Therefore, "*With the data available at the time of the study, and at an alpha of 0.05, I reject the null hypothesis. The gender of the driver of the vehicle does appear to influence the issuance of a traffic citation.*"

The Phi Coefficient

Now that we have determined whether the relationship between the variables was statistically significant or not using the chi-square test, we are ready to measure the strength of that relationship. If we developed our chi-square table as a 2X2 table (two rows and two columns; read as two-by-two), we would use a test known as the Phi Coefficient. The formula is relatively simple and makes use of the <u>computed</u> chi-square value. *Be sure when you work this formula you use the value you computed for chi-square, not the value from the table.*

$$\phi = \sqrt{\frac{\chi^2}{N}}$$

When we run the Phi Coefficient, we will get a number that will fall somewhere between 0 and 1. If we return a "0," this tells us that there is no relationship between the independent and dependent variables. If we return a "1," we know that the relationship is perfect. While it is possible to get a "0" or a "1" when you perform this test of strength, it is most likely that you will end up with a number somewhere between the two extremes. As an example, let's say you have run the formula for the Phi Coefficient and now have an end result of 0.15. Since 0.15 is pretty close to "0," we would know that we have a very weak relationship and would state so in our report. If, on the other hand, we ended up with a Phi Coefficient of 0.80, we would have a fairly strong relationship between the dependent and independent variables. You make the call on the strength of the relationship depending upon where between 0 and 1 your computed Phi Coefficient falls.

As an example, let's go back to the 2X2 table we developed a few pages ago concerning gender and whether or not the person had been drinking prior to when the officers arrived. When we compute our chi-square, we get 1.266 (0.205 + 0.290 + 0.321 + 0.450 = 1.266). And, a 2X2 (two-by-two) table would give us one (1) degree of freedom (number of rows minus one times the number of columns minus one). So, with one degree of freedom and an alpha of

0.05, the chi-square table provided a critical value of 3.841. Comparing our computed chi-square of 1.266, we see that the difference between males and females concerning whether they had been drinking or not is not statistically significant. So we would, with the data available to us at the time of the test and using an alpha value of 0.05, fail to reject the null hypothesis; gender does not appear to influence whether or not the subjects had been drinking prior to the arrival of the officers.

When we test the strength of the relationship of our variables, using the Phi Coefficient (since this is a 2X2 table) we find the result is 0.101, or a very weak relationship.

$$\phi = \sqrt{\frac{1.266}{123}} = \sqrt{0.0103}$$

$$\phi = 0.101$$

Cramér Coefficient V

If you are working with a table that is larger than a 2X2, say a 2X3 or maybe a 3X5, you would measure the strength of the relationship between the dependent and independent variables using a test known as the Cramér Coefficient V.

$$V = \sqrt{\frac{\chi^2}{N(J-1)}}$$

You have probably noticed this formula is almost the same as the formula for the Phi Coefficient; the only difference is the addition of $(J-1)$. $J-1$ tells you to take the number of rows, or the number of columns, <u>whichever is smaller</u>, and subtract 1. Once you have done this, you multiply that result by N and complete the formula. As an example, if you had two columns and three rows, you would subtract one from two (because two is smaller than three) and have one $(2-1=1)$. You would then multiply N times one and complete the formula; three columns and five rows would produce $3-1=2$. If N was 15, the result for the bottom half of the formula would be 30. If the number of columns and rows are the same, let's say 3X3, then you simply subtract one ($3 - 1 = 2$) and multiply N times 2 (if N is 23, then you would have $23 \times 2 = 46$).

Once you have worked the formula to this point, you simply complete the math by dividing your <u>computed</u> chi-square (not the table chi-square) by N ($J - 1$) and then hit the square root key on your calculator.

Just like the Phi Coefficient, the result will fall between 0 and 1. It is then up to you to interpret the result of your test. You should be aware, however, that in the Cramér's Coefficient V it is possible for the result of your test of the relationship between the variables to equal a perfect relationship (1), even though the data in your table does not appear to be perfectly related. This can happen when there are more rows than columns, and at least one of your independent variables (those across the top of the table) is associated with more than one of the dependent variables (those along the side of your table). As an example, the independent variables might be deputy sheriff and city officer. The dependent variables might be verbal warning, written warning, citation, and arrest.

While this is an extreme (and made-up) example, it shows us that in situations where each independent variable is associated with at least two dependent variables a perfect relationship could be portrayed, even though it may not seem perfect when we simply look at our table. Remember, normally a perfect relationship is found when the dependent variable relies completely on the independent variable. And, the larger (closer to 1) the result of either the Phi Coefficient or Cramér's Coefficient V, the stronger the relationship between the variables in your contingency table.

Now, let's use the Excel program to check our work and find the alpha value. Remember, for us to declare that we have a significant difference in our data (it is not just happening by chance), we need to have a returned alpha value of 0.05 or less (≤ 0.05).

First, we need to open an Excel data sheet and place our observed values in one row (the top row) and the expected values in the second row (the bottom row). See Figure 5.7.

Figure 5.7

48	56	148	128	125	63
59	45	133	120	106	82

Now, with this information in our data sheet, look to the top at the bar and select the "Formulas" tab. Then go over and click on the "More Functions," then click on "Statistical."

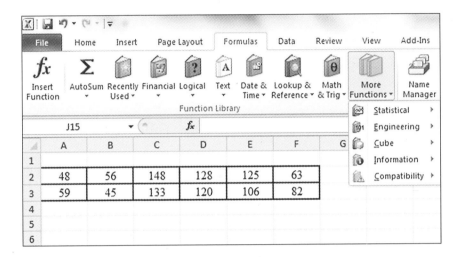

Next, scroll down the list of test until you see "CHISQ.TEST," then click on this tab and a window will open that is titled "Function Arguments." In this window you will see a rectangle that asks for the "Actual Range" and the "Expected Range."

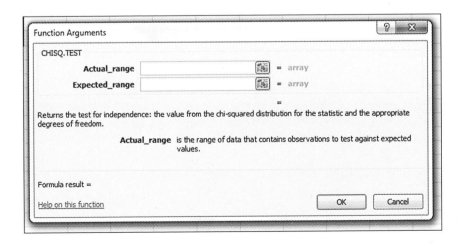

With your vertical line blinking in the rectangle labeled "Actual Range," point your cursor at the cell with 48 in it, hold the left mouse button down, and drag the cursor to the right until you have enclosed the row of data running from 48 on the left to 63 on the right. Release your left mouse button, and the cell descriptions should now be flashing in the rectangle asking for the "Actual Range." Now, click in the rectangle that is asking for the "Expected Range," and a vertical line should start flashing in this rectangle. Point your cursor at the second line of data (the expected values) in the cell with the value of 59, hold the left mouse button down and drag the cursor to the right to enclose the cell with the value of 82. The cell description of the expected values should now be showing in the Expected Range rectangle.

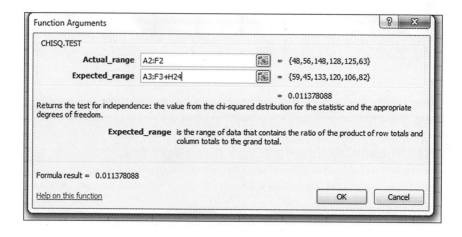

We are now at the last step of understanding whether or not our data demonstrates a statistically significant finding. Look at the lower left of the window, and you will see where it says "Formula result = 0.011378088." This number represents the alpha value of our chi-square test. If we round this number, we would have 0.01. To have a significant finding, we need an alpha of 0.05 or less, and 0.01 is less than 0.05, so we do indeed have a significant finding and may reject the null hypothesis.

Chapter Six

Learning How to Make Use of Correlations

Correlation

When you are working with correlations, you are reviewing the relationship between two or more ratio variables. As an example, if you are responsible for a fleet of vehicles, you might be interested in the relationship between the weight of the vehicle and the gas mileage. Common sense would tell us that the heavier the vehicle the lower the gas mileage should be. But this is not always true as other factors may be involved that would affect the gas mileage of the vehicle. While there is obviously an association between the weight of the vehicle and the gas mileage, we really need to be more precise in our understanding of that relationship.

The above example is a simple one, and when you work with and manage people, the relationships between variables may be very complicated. The use of *correlation* will provide a tool that we may apply to provide a better understanding of the direction and strength of relationships between variables.

How to Plot Data

When we are working with two variables, perhaps the weight and gasoline mileage of vehicles, we say that we are performing a bivariate analysis. An easy way to remember this term is to think of a bicycle ("bi": two wheels) and the fact that we are doing an analysis of what we observed (the two variables), thus, *bivariate analysis*. As we prepare to do our analysis, we need to designate one of the variables as X and the other variable as Y. Keep in mind that we are thinking that the X variable (the predictor or independent variable) is going to have some type of an influence on the Y variable (the dependent vari-

57

able). In our example, we could assume that the weight of the vehicle would have an impact on the gas mileage, so we will designate the weight of the vehicle as the X variable and the gas mileage as the Y variable.

The first thing that we want to do is arrange our data so that it will be more useful and easier to work with. In order to do this, we are going to create a table in which we have arranged the data in a format known as a *bivariate distribution*. In other words, we have two variables, and we have placed them into a table format that shows how they are distributed. While it is true that our data is now better organized than in a raw state, our table still does not give us a great deal of information in regard to the relationship between variable X (weight of vehicle) and variable Y (gas mileage). See Figure 6.1.

Figure 6.1 · Weight of Vehicle and Miles Per Gallon

Vehicle	Vehicle Weight (in pounds)	Miles per Gallon
A	3,500	21
B	3,200	23
C	4,300	18
D	3,300	21
E	4,150	19
F	3,800	20
G	2,900	24
H	3,100	23
I	3,000	22

A very simple way to tell if there appears to be a relationship between variable X and variable Y is to use the data to create a *scatter diagram*. As you can see in the example shown below, the X variable (weight of vehicle) has been arranged across the bottom, or horizontal axis, of the scatter diagram in 500-pound increments; the Y variable has been arranged along the side, or vertical axis, in increments of 5 miles. In statistical terms, the Y axis is referred to as the *ordinate* while the X axis is called the *abscissa* (Lurigio, et al., 1997). See Figure 6.2.

Notice in the chart above that the data points, each representing a vehicle, have developed a pattern that slopes downward from left to right. They are also fairly

Figure 6.2

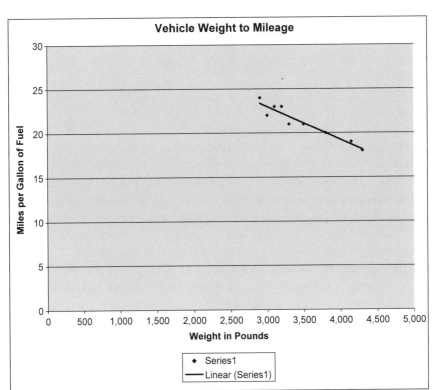

closely grouped around a line that we have inserted that is referred to as a *trend line*. The downward angle, from left to right, tells us that the relationship between the weight of the vehicle and the miles per gallon has an inverse, or negative, relationship: When the weight goes up, the overall trend is for the fuel mileage to go down. Also, the fact that the data points are clustered pretty closely around the trend line indicates that the data is pretty solid; there is not much variance in the relationship between weight and mileage and the various vehicles.

While most computer programs will create a scatter diagram for you (you may also hear them referred to as *scatterplots* or *scattergrams*), it is possible to create one by hand without too much work, depending upon how much data you are working with. By studying the example above, you will notice that all you have to do is take one entry at a time (one vehicle in this case) and find where the weight of the vehicle would be along your horizontal (bottom) axis. You would then lightly draw a vertical line with a pencil (so you can erase it later) from this point upward toward the top of your scatter diagram. Next, you would find the gas mileage <u>for this same vehicle</u> along the side (vertical) axis and then lightly draw a pencil line straight out from that point going to the right. Where these two pencil lines intersect, or cross each other, is where you would make a permanent mark. Each mark you make on your diagram represents the relationship of weight and gas mileage for that particular vehicle.

Covariation

The scatter diagram is a visual representation of the relationships found within your data for the variables we are presently concerned with. If you look carefully at the scatter diagram, you will notice that the data points we plotted tend to vary together in a particular way, in effect developing a pattern we can readily see (most of the time). In statistics, when our dots tend to change with each other, we say that they *covary* (co-vary). Thus, the term *covariation* is just another way of saying that as change occurs in one variable (X), we can expect to see change in the other variable (Y).

As you review the scatter diagram above, you should be able to see a pattern of relationship between the weight of the vehicle and the gas mileage. Generally, as the weight of the car goes up, the gas mileage will go down. We say "generally" because this is not true in every case; there could be a case where the gas mileage goes up with a heavier car, but generally speaking, it will go down. Also, you will notice that within the pattern of the data plot there will be a general direction of movement (most of the time) either upward or downward as your plot progresses across your scatter diagram (in our example, the direction is downward toward the right lower corner).

The pattern that we produce when we plot our data will give us a general feel for the direction of movement and the strength of the relationship between our variables. If we detect a movement that is upward, we know we have a positive relationship between the variables. In a positive relationship, as the value of one variable increases, so does the value of the other variable. If, on the other hand, we can detect a downward movement to our plot, we know that we have a negative, or inverse, relationship between our variables. In an inverse relationship (which we have in our example), as the value of one variable increases (the weight of the vehicle), the value of the other variable decreases (gas mileage).

Our scatter diagram will also provide information as to the strength of the relationship between our two variables. As our plot moves across the page, it will generally move either in an upward or downward direction. The sharper the angle of movement, the greater the affect of variable X on variable Y. If our dots more-or-less track straight across the page, this would tend to tell us that variable X is not really exerting much influence on variable Y.

As we observe our plotted data, we will also want to notice how spread out the points are as they make their movement either upward or downward (we assume influence in this example). If we were to take a ruler and draw a line right through the middle of the points of data, from one side of the plot to the other, we would be roughly tracking the average, or mean progression, in the relationship between the weight of the vehicle (X) and the gas mileage (Y). If we did this (and most computer programs will do this automatically for you if you want them to), we would notice that our individual dots fall either above or below our line, some of them closer to it and some farther away. Some data points might even be right on the trend line. The distance between our individual data points and the trend line is referred to as *deviation*. Those points that are above the line are positive (more miles-per-gallon than average for that weight of vehicle), and those found below the line are negative (less miles-per-gallon for that weight of vehicle). The less spread out above and below the trend line our data points are, the less variation (deviation) we have in our data.

In statistics we begin our mathematical investigation of the strength of the relationship by calculating the covariation between our two variables (the weight of the vehicle and the gas mileage for that vehicle). In order to do this we must find the deviation scores in every pair of measurements (a certain vehicle's weight and that same vehicle's gas mileage). Although this may be starting to sound confusing, keep in mind all that we are doing is finding the difference between a given dot on our scatter diagram and the line that represents the mean for our data as we move through the different vehicle weights and mileage measurements (just what we were talking about above).

A formula will provide direction to us as we calculate the covariation.

$$\text{Covariation} = \Sigma(X - \overline{X})(Y - \overline{Y})$$

Formulas are really easy to follow; all you have to do is break them into their various parts and then do what they tell you to do. Even those formulas that look very complicated and long can be easily worked if you do not get all excited, but rather take your time and simply break them into parts.

You can follow along on the example below as we work the covariation on vehicle weight and gas mileage. As you can see, the formula tells us what we will need in order to work it. It tells us we need to find the mean weight of all of our vehicles and the mean gas mileage. You already know how to do this, so for practice, go ahead and compute the means (average weight of our vehicles and the average gas mileage) and then check yourself with our example.

Once you have computed the average weight of our vehicles, you subtract that average weight from the individual weight of each vehicle. You then subtract the average miles-per-gallon from the miles-per-gallon shown for each individual vehicle, creating the table you see below. You will notice that we call the result of the calculations we just performed the *deviation score*. See Figure 6.3.

Now that we have created the deviation scores for our data, we are in the position to continue to the next step and create the *cross product* column. All you have to do to create this column is to multiply the X deviation score for each vehicle by that vehicle's Y deviation score. When you are done creating this column, sum (add) it to develop a *sum of the cross products* (in this case, −6,908.12). If the sum of the cross products is a positive number, we know that the relationship between our two variables is a positive one (they both move in the same direction). If the sum of our cross products is a negative number, we know that the relationship between our two variables is a nega-

Figure 6.3 · Weight of Vehicle and Miles Per Gallon
Covariation

Vehicle	Vehicle Weight (in pounds)	Mean	Deviation	Miles per Gallon	Mean	Deviation	$\Sigma (X - \bar{X})(Y - \bar{Y})$
	X			Y			
A	3,500	3,472	28	21	21.22	−0.22	−6.16
B	3,200	3,472	−272	23	21.22	1.78	−484.16
C	4,300	3,472	828	18	21.22	−3.22	−2,666.16
D	3,300	3,472	−172	21	21.22	−0.22	37.84
E	4,150	3,472	678	19	21.22	−2.22	−1,505.16
F	3,800	3,472	328	20	21.22	−1.22	−400.16
G	2,900	3,472	−572	24	21.22	2.78	−1,590.16
H	3,100	3,472	−372	23	21.22	1.78	−662.16
I	3,000	3,472	472	22	21.22	0.78	368.16
							−6,908.12

tive one (when one goes up, the other goes down). The larger the number representing the sum of our cross products column, the more strongly related the variables will appear to be. If the sum of the cross products column is very small, or maybe even zero, this would tell us that the variables do not appear to be related.

An important point to keep in mind is that the cross products method of evaluating the relationship between our two variables is a rough guide, which is influenced by the size of the data pool with which we are working. With a large data pool, the sum of the cross products column will naturally be larger, not necessarily because the relationship is stronger, but just because we are adding so many numbers together. With a smaller data pool, we will have a lower sum of the cross products column, not necessarily because the relationship is weaker, but simply due to the addition of fewer numbers.

However, there is a way to control for the size of the data pool and that is to find the average (mean) of the sum of the cross products. We do this by following the formula for covariation.

$$\text{Cov(x,y)} = \frac{\Sigma(X - \overline{X})(Y - \overline{Y})}{N - 1}$$

You can see that the formula tells us to divide the sum of the cross products column by $N - 1$. $N - 1$ is the number of persons, places, or things in our data minus one. Subtracting one off the total number of vehicles in our data provides a more accurate result when working with a sample then dividing by N.

Thus, we take $-6,908.12$ and divide by 8 (9 vehicles $- 1$) and get -863.52. The result is still a large number, and negative, so we know there appears to be a fairly strong inverse relationship between the variables.

Pearson Product-Moment Correlation

Now that we understand covariation, we are ready to take the next step and learn how to calculate and evaluate the *Pearson Product-Moment Correlation*. While covariation is useful in helping us understand the extent of the relationship of two variables (how much they vary together to be exact), a problem exists in that we are still carrying the measurements of our two variables (weight and miles-per-gallon in our example). This is, because, when we multiply our X deviation scores by our Y deviation scores, we are eventually creating a sum of the cross products that is in a measurement of weight-miles-per-gallon (really hard to make sense out of this one).

To solve this problem, we turn to the Pearson Product-Moment Correlation. The complete explanation of how this works is better suited to a more in-depth statistical class. For our purposes, it is enough to know when to use this correlation and understand how to calculate the formula, which is:

$$r = \frac{N \Sigma X Y - (\Sigma X)(\Sigma Y)}{\sqrt{[N \Sigma X^2 - (\Sigma X)^2][N \Sigma Y^2 - (\Sigma Y)^2]}}$$

The first thing you need to do to work this formula is to take a deep breath and relax. Remember, we are going to break it into parts and work one part at a time. Working a formula is just like reading a recipe to bake a cake. The first thing you do when you bake a cake is to read the recipe and see what ingredients you will need to have ready before you start the actual process of mixing the cake batter. Likewise, if you look carefully at the Pearson formula, you will know what you have to do in advance to make the whole process much easier. We will lay our information out in columns as we move along through the formula. Using a column format will make the process very clear, and it will be much easier to go back and verify our results if we should question our end product.

The first column contains the vehicle identification; perhaps we have numbered the vehicles so we can tell them apart. The second column is the X column and contains the actual weight of each vehicle as it is matched to the vehicle designation. The third column is the Y column and contains the actual average miles-per-gallon for this particular designated vehicle. We create the fourth column by going back to the X column and multiplying each vehicle weight by itself; this is read as X-squared. The fifth column is created the same way, except now we are squaring the entries in our Y column (miles-per-gallon); this is read as Y-squared. The sixth and final column is the result of multiplying each individual X column entry by its corresponding Y column entry (the weight of each individual vehicle by its own average gas mileage). Now that you have created all of the columns, sum (add) them and record the totals somewhere below the proper column for use in completing the formula. See Figure 6.4.

Now that we have all of the ingredients in order, it is time to actually work the formula. We will look at the portion of the formula located above the horizontal line first. But before we get to work, we should discuss how we know

Figure 6.4 · Weight of Vehicle and Miles Per Gallon
Pearson Product-Moment Correlation

Vehicle	Vehicle Weight (in pounds)	Miles per Gallon			
	X	Y	X^2	Y^2	XY
A	3,500	21	12,250,000	441	73,500
B	3,200	23	10,240,000	529	73,600
C	4,300	18	18,490,000	324	77,400
D	3,300	21	10,890,000	441	69,300
E	4,150	19	17,222,500	361	78,850
F	3,800	20	14,440,000	400	76,000
G	2,900	24	8,410,000	576	69,600
H	3,100	23	9,610,000	529	71,300
I	3,000	22	9,000,000	484	66,000
	31,250	191	110,552,500	4,085	655,550

when to do what. We are going to be multiplying, dividing, adding, and subtracting. When you see two letters together (XY) this tells us to multiply X times Y. When you see the little mark that looks like a misshaped E you know to sum (add). If you see a letter inside of parentheses (ΣX), you perform that action separately. In this case we are told to sum the X column (which we have already done). (ΣX) (ΣY) tells us to multiply the sum of the X column by the sum of the Y column. If you do not see any other marks, you will multiply. As an example, NΣXY tells us to multiply N times the sum of the X multiplied by Y column.

The formula tells us to take N (the number of vehicles in our data) and multiply that number by the sum (Σ; total) of our XY (X times Y) column. Since we already know the result of the sum of the XY column, it is easy to plug this information into the formula (actually, replace the formula with the numbers as we work along). Next, the formula tells us to subtract the sum (Σ) of the X column multiplied by the sum (Σ) of the Y column. So multiply the sum of the X column by the sum of the Y column, and then take that result and place it into the formula, so we can subtract it when we are ready to do so.

It is now time to move to the lower portion of the formula, continuing to replace the formula with numbers. Notice the bottom portion of the formula is really in two parts, each part encapsulated by brackets. You work each section in brackets separately, just as you work the portions of the formula that are enclosed in parentheses separately. The first set of brackets tells us to take N and multiply it by the sum (Σ) of the X-squared (X^2) column, then to subtract the sum (Σ) of the X column, which we have squared ($\Sigma X)^2$. <u>You must be very careful not be confuse which X column we are working with</u>. One is a column of X that we simply have summed. The other is the column where we squared our X value to create a separate column of X squared (X^2). At this point in the formula, we are taking the sum of the first column, the X column, and squaring only the sum. You can tell this by looking at where the "little 2" (2) is located in the formula. If it is right next to a letter, it tells you that you are working with that letter after you have squared it. If it is separated from the letter by parentheses, it is telling you that you sum the column first, then square only the sum ($\Sigma X)^2$.

Now we are ready to move on to the second set of brackets. Here we are told to multiply N by the sum of our Y-squared column ($N\Sigma Y^2$), then to subtract the sum of our Y column, which we have squared (squaring only the sum of this column) ($\Sigma Y)^2$.

Let's continue to work the formula. Remember, you do all of the math above the horizontal line, then all the math below the line. Check yourself once again by referring to the example below.

$$\frac{9(655,550)-(31,250)(191)}{\sqrt{[9(110,552,500)-976,562,500][9(4,085)-36,481]}}$$

$$\frac{5,899,950-5,968,750}{\sqrt{(18,410,000)(284)}}$$

$$\frac{-68,800}{\sqrt{5,228,440,000}}$$

$$\frac{-68,800}{7230.795} = -.9515$$

We are now down to the final calculations in our Pearson Product-Moment Correlation. Looking at the formula, you will notice something that looks like this:

This tells you that you are going to find the square root of whatever is underneath this sign. In the case of the Pearson Product-Moment Correlation, the sign covers the entire bottom portion of the formula. So you do the math required in the bottom portion first. When you are all done, you would hit the square root key on your calculator. So we do the final math above the horizontal line and then divide that result by the square root of the result of all of the math below the horizontal line in the formula. To check yourself for the final time, see the example below.

Pearson Product-Moment as a Measure of Association

The correlation coefficient provides us with an indication of the strength and direction of the relationship between our variables. Since the correlation coefficient is a pure number, we do not have to worry about the problem of units that we discussed under covariation. If our calculated r (r is used to represent the Pearson Product-Moment Correlation) is a positive number (0.78, as an example), we know that the relationship between the variables is also positive. In other words, they both move in the same direction. If our calculated r is a negative number (–0.63, as an example), we know that this is a negative or inverse relationship. In other words, as one variable moves up in value, the other moves down. In the problem we worked above, r = –0.9515, or –0.952.

The number we produce when we performed the calculation to find the Pearson Product-Moment is referred to as its value. The value will run from –1.00 to +1.00. The closer the value is to 1.00, the stronger the relationship;

the closer the value is to 0.0, the weaker the relationship. In our example, we calculated –0.952, which is a very strong relationship, and since it is a negative number, we know that the relationship is negative or inverse (when one value goes up, the other value goes down).

Keep in mind that the value can never exceed 1, as 1 represents a perfect relationship (for every movement of a unit of one variable, there is an equal corresponding movement of a unit of the other variable). This 1-to-1 perfect relationship would produce a perfect linear relationship (a straight-line relationship) at a 45° angle. In other words, if r = 1, the data points would fall in a perfectly straight line. As the measurement moves further away from 1 (i.e., the measurement is moving toward 0), the data points will appear more scattered on the graph.

There is one more important thing to remember at this point. The strength of the relationship is represented by the closeness of the number to 1, not by the positive or negative sign. A common mistake that people make when learning Pearson's Product-Moment Correlation is to think that +0.23 represents a stronger relationship than –0.36. Not true! Forget the sign when looking for the strength of the relationship and consider that 0.36 is closer to 1 than 0.23, so the relationship is stronger. While both numbers demonstrate a weak relationship, we could say that 0.23 is very weak and 0.36 is simply weak. If we had a value of 0.42, we might designate it as a moderately weak relationship.

There is an easy way to determine the size of the correlation coefficient, and that is to square the number (r^2). When we square the number (the value of r), the result tells us the percentage of the dependent variable (Y), that is explained by its linear relationship with the other variable (X), the predictor variable. As an example, it we calculated an r of 0.83 and then squared it (r^2), we would come up with 0.6889, or 0.69. This tells us that 69% of the variance (movement) we see in the Y variable is caused by the relationship with the X variable. Remember that when you square a value, you will automatically remove the negative sign, so you will need to look at the original value to check to see if it is a positive or negative relationship. On our example from above, with an r of 0.952, we find that 0.906, or 90.6% of the movement in variable Y (miles per gallon) is explained by variable X (weight of the vehicle).

One last point before we move on to learn how to test the significance of r. Be sure that you check for outliers! Outliers, as you remember, are those scores that are to the extreme, either positive or negative. The outliers are so far away from the other scores that they will cause your r and r^2 to be distorted. You may wish to remove outliers before doing your computations. And, if you do, you should be sure to note this fact, so your readers will understand that you have disregarded the outlying scores.

Testing for the Statistical Significance of r

In order to test for statistical significance, we must first develop a null and alternative hypothesis. Of course, you remember from your earlier work in this text that you always test the null hypothesis. You will notice as you continue to read texts on statistics that if you are working with a population and testing r, the letter p (lower case Greek letter rho) is used to represent the population correlation coefficient.

Once your hypothesis is developed, you must have some way of deciding if the relationship is large enough to be significant (mean anything). Normally, the level of statistical significance we are looking for is a confidence level of 0.05. But as you remember, you may adjust this down (numbers below 0.05; 0.01 for example) to make the results even more significant by raising the bar of proof, or up (numbers higher than 0.05; 0.10 for example) to make it easier to declare significance by lowering the bar of proof. If the alpha number goes up, say to 0.10, the level of proof needed to declare significance goes down; if the alpha goes down, perhaps to 0.01, the level of proof needed to declare significance does up. This may seem a little confusing at first, but sit back and think about it for a few minutes, and it will make sense.

To determine if your r is statistically significant (and if it is, you may reject the null hypothesis), you need to consult a table of critical values for the correlation coefficient (see table in the rear of this text). In order to use the table, you will need to know the degrees of freedom for your data. To find the degrees of freedom, you will take the number of individuals (things) in your study and subtract two. To use the table, you go down the left column (marked as df) until you find the correct degrees of freedom. You then come across to your right until you are in the column representing the desired level of significance. There are two things to keep in mind as you do this: (1) 0.05 is the standard that is most often used, and (2) you may run either a one-tailed or a two-tailed test.

If you can anticipate a direction of movement in your data, either up or down, you may use the one-tailed column. If you are not able to anticipate a direction of movement, you should use the two-tailed column. As an example, if you have 10 degrees of freedom, the critical value for an alpha level of 0.05 in a two-tailed test would be 0.576, but only 0.497 in a one-tailed test. Thus, if you had a calculated r of 0.521, it would be a significance finding in a one-tailed test, but not if you were running a two-tailed test. If your test proves a statistical significance, you "reject the null hypothesis." If your r fails to test as statistically significant, you "fail to reject the null hypothesis." As you remember, using an alpha level of 0.05 to find critical values means that out of 100 samples we could expect to find such a significant result less than 5 times purely by chance. Also, you may always run a two-tailed test (many statisticians prefer to do so) as it provides a higher bar of proof to declare significance.

Two last points to make before we move on to linear regression. Keep in mind that Pearson's r was designed to measure straight-line relationships (linear) and that other relationships do exist. There are relationships that will look like a mountain when they are plotted—starting low, peaking, and the returning to the bottom of the plot. Relationships that plot this way are called *curvilinear*. As an example, students who take aspirin for a headache, often caused by stats exams, find that the level of relief goes up as they take more aspirin but only to a point, after which the headache relief actually declines with respect to the number of aspirin taken. Perhaps it would help if I referred to this as akin to the "law of diminishing returns" where the situation gets better to a point and then it does not seem to help much more as you continue to put in more and more effort.

Also, the size of your sample will affect the value of your r. If you look at the table for critical values for the correlation coefficient, you will notice that as the degrees of freedom get larger, which indicates a larger and larger sample size, progressively smaller values of r are needed to obtain statistical significance. Thus, a larger sample, which by itself would provide a greater degree of accuracy, will require a lower bar of proof to declare statistical significance.

Using Excel to Compute Our r

The first thing you need to do is enter your data in an Excel spreadsheet in two columns, with the predictor variables (X variables) in one column and the dependent variables (Y variables) in a second column. It is possible that you may have more than two variables, but for the sake of learning how to do this, two is enough.

Once you have your variables entered, look to the top of the Excel spreadsheet and click on "Data," and then look to the right and click on "Data Analysis." A window is going to open, and you need to select "Correlation," then click "OK."

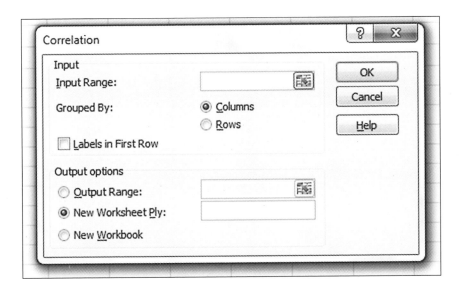

A new window will now open, and it is asking where the data is. Place the cursor at the upper left corner of the first column of data, hold down on the left mouse button, and then drag the cursor to the lower right corner of the data before releasing the mouse button. You should now see a flashing line around the data, and the cell designations should appear in the little rectangular window. Remember, if you have labeled your columns, which I think is always a good idea, you need to click the little box that tells the program that you have labels included in the encapsulated data.

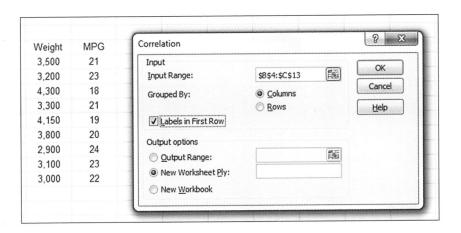

The last step is to click "OK." The program will now calculate and provide the r value that you need in order to determine the Pearson Product Moment Correlation and the strength of the relationship between the variables.

Chapter Seven

Making Application of Simple Linear Regression

You are already an expert at making predictions. It is your ability to predict what will happen that allows you to function effectively in your everyday life. You predict that the other vehicle will obey the traffic laws and the behavior of other people as you meet them over the course of the day. If you had to analyze every situation before you yourself acted, you would not mentally survive the day.

Making some type of prediction is essential to many of the activities in the criminal justice profession. Whether you are forecasting the activity of your department, the use of your vehicles, the morale of your officers, or the allocation of resources, you will make better decisions if you have the ability to look into the future with a certain level of accuracy.

The Basics and the Terminology

As we move into regression we will begin by working with *simple* or *bivariate regression*. As you remember, "bi" tips us that we will be working with two of something, like the word "bicycle" tells us to expect to see two wheels on the vehicle. By using regression, we are able to make a prediction as to what we think will happen to the outcome variable (Y) based upon its linear relationship with the second variable (X), the predictor variable.

In order for a variable to work in regression, that variable must be measurable, at least on the interval scale, and the two (or more) variables must somehow be related to each other. We refer to this relationship as a *linear relationship*, and if our prediction is to be valid, we must assume the assumptions of measurement and relationship are met.

It may be helpful, as we get started in this section, to think of a linear relationship in a visual sense. Try to picture your data as dots entered upon a scatter diagram, the X variable plotted on the horizontal axis (running left to right) and the Y variable plotted on the vertical axis (running up and down the page). As we plot our data, we are in effect placing it in a visual order with each related X and Y variable plotted to develop a dot at a specific point in our scatter diagram (*known as ordered pairs*). In other words, if we were plotting height and weight, assuming that height and weight are related and height normally predicts the weight of an individual, we would plot the height across the horizontal axis (X variable) and weight up the vertical axis (Y variable). If the individual (an element in our sample) was 68 inches tall, we would locate where 68 inches would be on the horizontal axis (our horizontal axis is in increments of inches) and, if the person was 170 pounds, where 170 pounds would be on the vertical axis (the vertical axis might be in increments of 5 pounds). We would then draw a line up from 68 and across from 170 to fix the data point, which represents this one individual element from our sample.

Generally speaking, once we have plotted all of our data points, and if we have a linear relationship between our two variables (ordered pairs), we will notice that we have formed a pattern of dots that will produce a straight-line movement. This pattern will not only tell us if a linear relationship exists, but also whether it is a positive or negative (inverse) relationship. Remember, this line may not be perfectly obvious, but if we look at the general pattern of the dots, we should be able to discern a pattern of movement. As a general example of a positive and fairly strong relationship between two variables, see Figure 7.1 below. Variable 1 would be the X (predictor) variable and Variable 2 would be the Y (dependent) variable.

Figure 7.1

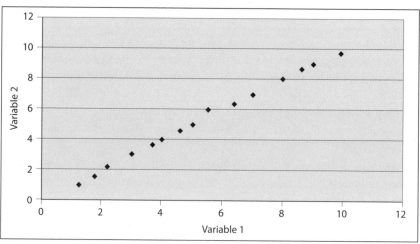

Source: www.statcan.ca/english.edu

As a review from Chapter Six, the formulas for correlation and simple regression look a little daunting at first, but, as we will see, as you break them into their component parts they are not really difficult to work at all.

$$r = \frac{N\Sigma(xy) - \Sigma(x)\Sigma(y).}{\sqrt{[N\Sigma x^2 - (\Sigma x)^2][N\Sigma y^2 - (\Sigma y)^2]}}$$

Remember, as you look at the correlation formula, you work it in sections (you may also follow along using the example below this explanation). We need to know if there is sufficient correlation between the variables (variable x and variable y) to make it worthwhile proceeding to regression. Let's start above the horizontal line with the part that reads:

$$N\Sigma(xy) - \Sigma(x)\Sigma(y).$$

This formula is telling us to take the "N" (or how many elements (people or things)) and to multiply it by the sum (or total) of the x times the y column (the x and the y are inside parentheses so we know that they are to multiplied together first then summed then multiplied by N). Note: when you do not see a sign telling you what to do between two symbols, $N\Sigma(xy)$, you multiply. In other words, we will take each x and multiply it by its paired y (68 times 170, as an example) to create a new column of data, which we will label as xy. Once we have done this, we add (or sum) the new column of xy and then multiply the result by N. Once you have done this, you plug this result into the formula.

Next you do the same thing with the notation $\Sigma(x)\Sigma(y)$. This notation tells us to sum the original x column and then multiply that result by the sum of the original y column. Once you have done this, plug the result into the formula.

Now it is time to move to below the horizontal line. The first thing we should notice is this sign:

This sign tells us that we will eventually be going to the square root of this section of computations. Also, we should note that we now have brackets in addition to parentheses. When you see brackets, you know they encompass work that will be applied in total. This will make more sense once we make our way through this section of the formula.

$$\sqrt{[N\Sigma x^2 - (\Sigma x)^2][N\Sigma y^2 - (\Sigma y)^2]}$$

First, we will do the computations within the first set of brackets. Notice that we are working with the predictor variable, the x variable. We are told to take N and multiply that number by the sum of x^2. To do this, you need to make an x^2 column. All you have to do is take your x column and square the numbers. You then take the column of squared numbers, sum it, and then multiply by N. Plug the result of these computations into your formula, and we are ready to move on to the second step within the first set of brackets. Notice that it tells us next to subtract the sum of x that is then squared $(\Sigma x)^2$. Be careful here; the exponent "2" is outside of the parentheses, so you sum the x column first and then square the result. DO NOT square each x value and then sum the column of squared x's. Once you have completed this step, plug the result into the equation. Now, move on to the second set of brackets. Here we are working with the second variable (the dependent variable or the y variable). Follow the same procedure you performed within the first set of brackets, except now we are working with the y data. After plugging all of the number in to the formula, we are ready to complete our computations.

As an example, let's correlate height and weight. Common sense would tell us that as a person becomes taller, he or she, in general, should weigh more (keeping in mind there are always exceptions). Since we assume height determines weight, in our example height would be the x variable (predictor) and weight would be the y variable (dependent). See Figure 7.2.

Figure 7.2

Subject	Height in Inches (x)		Weight in Pounds (y)		
	(x)	(x)²	(y)	(y)²	(xy)
1	63	3,969	125	15,625	7,875
2	67	4,489	138	19,044	9,246
3	59	3,481	115	13,225	6,785
4	68	4,624	145	21,025	9,860
5	72	5,184	168	28,224	12,096
6	75	5,625	177	31,329	13,275
	404	27,372	868	128,472	59,137

$$\frac{6\,(59{,}137) - (404)\,(868)}{\sqrt{[6\,(27{,}372) - (404)^2]\,[6\,(128{,}472) - (868)^2]}}$$

$$\frac{4{,}150}{\sqrt{[1{,}016]\,[17{,}408]}}$$

$$r = 4{,}150 \,/\, 4{,}205.54$$
$$r = .987$$

We now know that our correlation between height and weight is 0.987 (rounding to three for convenience), which is a pretty strong positive correlation. Remember from our earlier work that a perfect correlation is either a +1 or a −1. As an additional check, we will want to go to the table for correlations in the back of the text and check for the critical value. Since we have 6 subjects in our sample (df = N − 2), we have 4 degrees of freedom. At 4 degrees of freedom and an alpha of 0.05, we would need a computed correlation of 0.729 or higher for our computation to be statistically significant. Since 0.987 is much higher than 0.729, we can safely state that we have statistical significance at the 0.05 level.

We are making good progress toward our simple regression. We have chosen variables that are at least on the interval level, and we have a significant correlation between the two variables. The last step is for us to demonstrate that our two variables have a linear relationship. A quick check is to use the Chart Wizard in Excel and plot our data points as discussed previously. Of course, we are looking for a clustering of the data that would indicate a general movement either up or down (in this case, since we have a positive correlation, we know the movement should be generally upward from left to right).

Linear Regression

Linear regression may be used to make predictions. By knowing what has happened in the past, we are in the position to make a good educated guess (with a certain amount of error) about what will happen in the future. As an example, using the data on height and weight, we would be able to predict the weight of someone if we knew their height. Of course, in our example, we only had six subjects, so our error will be fairly large. If we had used a larger sample of suspects, the error in our prediction would be smaller.

The formula used when there is only one x variable (the predictor) and one y variable (the dependent) with a linear relationship (straight line) is shown below and is known as *simple linear regression*.

$$Y = bx + a$$

Y is what we are trying to predict and is often shown (since it is an estimate) with a tilde (~) over the Y. The "b" represents the slope of the straight line that would form if we drew a line precisely through the middle of our data points following the general direction of movement of those points. The "x" represents that "unknown" value we want to plug into our formula to make our prediction (in the case above, we would plug in the height in inches of our new person in order to predict his or her weight). The "a" is the "constant," which is where our sloping line would cross the vertical line on our graph if the person were "0" inches tall.

There are ways to make regression predictions, even if the regression line is not a straight one, but that technique is more advanced and outside the scope of this text. For now, let's develop our simple regression line by continuing on with the height and weight example from above. We need to go back to a couple of simple formulas in order to know how, where, and when to use our data.

$$b = \frac{N\Sigma xy - (\Sigma x)(\Sigma y)}{N\Sigma x^2 - (\Sigma x)^2}$$

$$a = \overline{Y} - b\overline{X}$$

The X and Y with the line over them are called X-bar and Y-bar. These two signs represent the mean (average) of the Y data and the X data. Therefore, if we go back to our height and weight data, we would develop our formulas like this:

$$b = \frac{6\,(59{,}137) - (404)\,(868)}{6\,(27{,}372) - 163{,}216}$$

$$b = \frac{354{,}822 - 350{,}672}{164{,}232 - 163{,}216}$$

$$b = \frac{4150}{1016}$$

$$b = 4.085$$

$$a = \overline{Y} - b\overline{X}$$

$$a = 144.667 - 4.085\,(67.333)$$

$$a = -130.388$$

Thus, our formula to predict the weight of someone who is 6' 3" tall (75") would be:

$$\tilde{Y} = bx + a$$

$$\tilde{Y} = 4.085\,(75) + -130.388$$

$$\tilde{Y} = 175.987, \text{ or } 176 \text{ pounds}$$

As you now see, regression really isn't that difficult, if we take the time to understand the process and break the equations into workable sections. Of course, we also know that, because we are making a prediction with error, our 6' 3" person will not weigh 176 pounds exactly but will be in the area of 176 pounds. It is possible to compute what our error is likely to be. With that knowledge, we will be able to develop a window into which the weight of our individual will fall with a stated degree of accuracy.

Determining the Accuracy of Our Prediction

The equation we will use to develop a measure of the amount of error in our prediction, once again, looks more difficult than it is once you understand what is going on. You might wonder how we can predict how much error we will encounter with our prediction if we are looking into the future. We are able to do this, quite naturally, by looking into the known data from past experience, our sample of six people in our height and weight example. Since we know how much each of them weighed and how tall they were, we use this data as a test of the accuracy of our regression model. To do this, we take the height of Subject One and try to predict his weight. Subject One was 63 inches tall. If we plug 63 into the regression formula we developed, we predict this person will weigh 126.967, or 127 pounds. We know from our data that Subject One actually weighed 125 pounds, thus we have an error of two pounds (rounded). We do this with every person or object in our sample to determine what turns out to be an averaged amount of error, known as the *standard error of estimate*. The distance from the actual weight (or whatever we are measuring) to our predicted weight (the error on this one data point) is called a *residual*. You will notice in the equation (below) that we are squaring our errors to avoid ending up with a "zero" when we are done summing them (remember the need to square from our earlier work in the text?). As you know, we are trying to place our sloping line (b) right down the middle of our data plot, thus minimizing our error as much as possible. Doing this is known in statistics as the *least-squares criterion*, or in plain English, placing our line in such a position as to cut the error in our calculations as much as possible with the data we have available (ending up with the smallest number possible when we summed the squared errors). This is why you will often see the sloping line we have developed referred to as the *best-fitting line*, or *line of best fit*. The equation for our error, the *standard error of estimate*, looks like this:

$$S_{s \cdot x} = \sqrt{\frac{\Sigma(\widetilde{Y} - y)^2}{N - 2}}$$

The first thing we should notice as we look at this equation is that after we have completed the computations, we need to hit the square root key on our calculator (remember, during the calculations, we are squaring our numbers to avoid ending up with a "zero," just like we did in variation and standard deviation). As we study the equation further, we should note that it tell us to take each of the actual "Y" values (the real weight of the subjects in our example) and subtract what we predicted the weight would be. Then we square the result. We do this with each and every one of the subjects in our example and then sum the squared results. Next, we divide by "N − 2," which in the case of our example would be 6 − 2 = 4. Then, as we already know, we hit the square root key. We now have calculated the *standard error of estimate* for a simple regression. We would like to have the standard error of estimate as small as possible because a smaller error means greater accuracy in our prediction. We would then add and subtract the standard error to and from our estimated Y value. We would predict the weight of a given subject to fall within the two limits with a certain amount of accuracy. If we wanted to predict with 95% accuracy, we would multiply the standard error by 1.96 and then add and subtract that figure from the predicted value of Y.

Remember, in order for our regression to work, we must have some correlation between the variables. If our correlation happened to be +1 or −1, our relationship would be perfect and there would be no error. If the correlation equals 0, there would be no relationship and no reason to continue. Of course, we would like to see a reasonably strong correlation between the two variables, as it allows us to be more accurate in our prediction.

The whole purpose of looking at prediction error is to determine how much better we are doing with our predictions, using regression, than we would do by simply taking the average of the group and predicting that everyone would fall at the average. In order to do this, we have to make our way through a few steps of calculations.

To review, we have to consider how much error we are making when we use X (the height of a subject, to continue using the example we started with) to predict Y (the weight of the person). We did this when we computed the *standard error of estimate*. First, simply put, if we have a group (sample) of ten people, we can actually measure their height and weight. We then use our regression formula to predict their weight, using their height. Once we have done this, we compare our predicted weight with the actual weight for each subject, find the difference, square it, and then sum the column. This sum is referred to as the *sum of the squared errors* and is noted as SSE

Next, we compute the amount of error, which would result from our prediction of weight, if we did not know anything about the variables that predict weight. As mentioned above, <u>if we do not know anything about predictor variables, the best we can do is use the average weight of the sample as our predicted weight for every new person about whom we wish to make a weight prediction</u>. To do this, we take the average (mean) weight of our sample of ten and subtract that mean weight from the actual weight of each person in our sample. Like we did before, we must square the difference for each one of these calculations in the new column of data we are forming, and then we sum the column of squared differences. This result, the sum of the column, is called the *total squared error* and is noted by SS_T.

Now we can apply the equation shown below to find the proportionate reduction in the error of our prediction, which will result if we use X (height) to predict Y (weight), rather than just using the average (mean) weight of the group as a predicted weight for every person (*proportionate reduction in prediction error*). See Figure 7.3.

$$\frac{SS_T - SS_E}{SS_T}$$

Figure 7.3

Subject	Actual Height (Inches)	Actual Weight (Pounds)	Predicted Weight	Differences	Differences Squared
	X	Y	$\tilde{Y}$	$Y - \tilde{Y}$	$(Y - \tilde{Y})^2$
1	68	155	160.79	−5.79	33.52
2	71	172	175.55	−3.55	12.6
3	65	149	146.03	2.97	8.82
4	74	180	190.31	−10.31	106.3
5	76	202	200.15	1.85	3.42
6	72	175	180.47	−5.47	29.92
7	66	155	150.95	4.05	16.4
8	78	215	209.99	5.01	25.1
9	75	200	195.23	4.77	22.75
10	70	177	170.63	6.37	40.58
SUM					299.41

$$S_{y \cdot x} = \sqrt{\frac{\Sigma (Y - \tilde{Y})^2}{N - 2}}$$

$$= \sqrt{\frac{299.41}{8}}$$

$$= 6.118$$

We now know that our standard error of estimate is 6.118 pounds. Therefore, we could predict that someone who was 71 inches tall would weigh 176 pounds. If we wanted to be able to say that we were 95% confident, we would multiply our standard error of estimate by 1.96 (z for 95%) and get 6.118(1.96) = 11.991, or 12 pounds. We would then predict that our subject would weigh between 164 and 188 pounds (rounded off).

To compute our proportionate reduction in error, we would simply plug in the column sums from the table below. See Figure 7.4.

Thus, since the proportionate reduction in error is the same as r^2, we know that almost 94% of the variance in weight is explained by the variable of height. Also, since 0.937 is well above 0.50, we know that it is much better to use our

Figure 7.4

Subject	Actual Weight	Minus Mean Squared	Minus Predicted Squared
1	155	529	33.52
2	172	36	12.6
3	149	841	8.82
4	180	64	106.3
5	202	576	3.42
6	175	9	29.92
7	155	529	16.4
8	215	1,369	5.01
9	200	484	22.75
10	177	1	40.58
Sum	1,780	4,438	279.32
Mean	178		

$$\frac{SS_T - SS_E}{SS_T}$$

$$= \frac{4438 - 279.32}{4438}$$

$$= .937$$

regression to predict the weight of subjects, based upon their height, than to simply use the mean weight and apply it to all subjects.

Using Excel to Perform a Regression

As we have done in previous chapters we need to enter our data in an Excel spreadsheet. Next, we click on "Data" and then "Data Analysis." We have performed these steps many times before, so I will not make screenshots of these steps at this time.

Now, in the window that opened when we clicked on "Data Analysis," scroll down and click on "Regression" and then click on "OK." A new window will open, and it is asking where our data is. It is important to notice that it is specifically asking for our "Y" data (the value we want to predict, and in our example that was weight) and the "X" data (the data we are using the make our prediction, the predictor variables(s), which in our example is height). Click and drag as we have done in our past chapters, and do not forget to check the little box and let the computer know if you have labels at the top of your columns. We do have some other features this time, as we can set select to do a confidence level as well as adjust what we want that confidence level to be. As you remember, 95% (which is the default) would give us a window that is two standard deviations above and below the mean of the data. Then we could say that we were 95% confident that the weight of a person 70 inches tall would fall between the high and low weights we predicted.

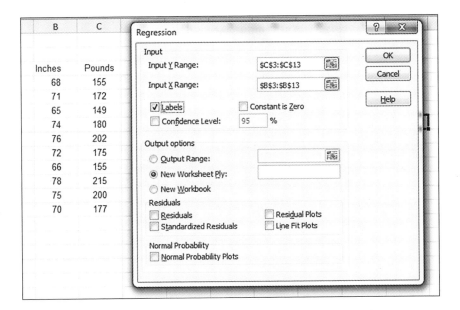

Another nice feature is that we can ask our program to figure the residuals and other interesting information for us, if we wish, by simply clicking in the appropriate little box. When we are ready to have our computer complete the work for us, click on "OK." Now, all we have to do is take a look at our data and perform our analysis and prediction of whatever it is that we are trying to predict. By the way, if we have more than one predictor (multiple regression), we do everything the same way; we just enclose all of the "X" data at once, as if it were all one very large column.

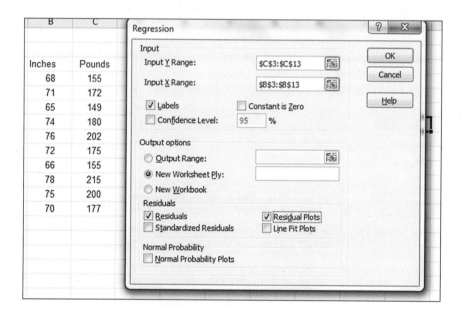

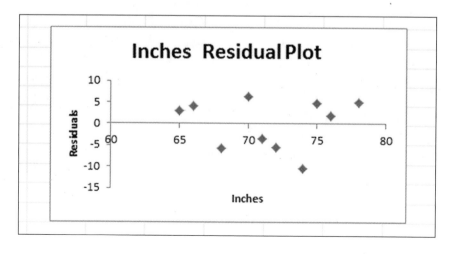

Chapter Eight

Multiple Regression Analysis

Moving from bivariate linear regression to multivariate regression (multiple regression), we are able to significantly increase our ability to make accurate predictions. This is so because we will use more than one predictor variable as we work our equation. While we could work the equation by hand, it would take a very long time, so we will be allowing the computer to do most of the work for us. However, we will review the process so that we will have a good solid understanding of what the computer is doing and how the output is calculated.

Just like simple regression, multiple regression uses *predictor variables* that produce a *criterion variable*. Rather than working with one predictor variable, however, one or more additional predictor variables are added to the mix to increase our accuracy. In order for multivariate regression to work, there are certain basic assumptions that must be met: (1) all predictor variables (X) are related to the criterion variable (Y), (2) there must be a linear relationship between the predictor variables and the criterion variable, and (3) all variables must be measurable on at least an interval scale.

In multiple regression, the predictor variables are weighted based upon their predictive ability. The purpose of weighting the predictor variables is to minimize the amount of error in our prediction. The computer does this by applying the *least squares criterion* to develop the weight (regression coefficients) that will minimize the squared differences between our predicted values and the actual values taken from our sample. In other words, the computer determines just how much each predictor variable contributes to the prediction we are making. Depending upon the amount of the contribution, each variable will be assigned a value (weight) within the multiple regression formula. The basic formula for multiple regression is really pretty easy to read.

$$\tilde{Y} = b_1 x_1 + b_2 x_2 + a$$

Notice that we are using the symbol (~) to denote that the Y value is a predicted value, not a known value. In order to make this prediction, the formula tells us to take the slope of the first predictor variable (b_1), which we have been able to compute using data from our sample, and to multiply the slope by the new, or unknown, value (x_1). If we are still trying to predict the weight of a person, we would take the value of the slope from our previous calculations (4.92) for height and multiply it by the height in inches of the person we would like to predict the weight of (just like we did before). Next, we take the slope of the second predictor value (b_2), also calculated from our sample, and multiply that value by the new, or unknown, value (x_2). As an example, suppose we decided to use the size of the waist of people in our sample as a predictor of their weight in addition to their height (more than one predictor variable = multivariate regression). We process this data just like we did the height to come up with the slope of the new predictor variable, the size of their waist in inches (b_2). Now when we try to predict the weight of someone, we also add the size of their waist in inches to our formula (x_2). The computed values of the predictor variables (b) are known as the *partial regression slopes* because each of them contributes part of the information we need to make our prediction of Y.

All that remains is to do the math with the predictor variables and then add the constant (point the intersecting line would cross the vertical), known as the value "a." The constant with the value "a," as you remember, is the intercept (or the point) where our sloping line intercepts the vertical line on a chart that represents the Y values, a point we refer to as the *Y intercept*. In multiple regression, this is the point on the vertical line (the Y line) of our chart that would be intersected by our sloping line "b" if the combined X values (X_1 and X_2) were zero (0). This should all sound very familiar to you as it is exactly the same concept as with simple regression; the only difference is that we are using more predictor variables.

Therefore, the slopes b_1 and b_2 (and other b values if we have additional predictor variables in our sample to work with) are the *weighted* values that permit us to calculate the value of Y based upon the unknown values of X_1 and X_2 (and perhaps other X values). Of course, we will know the values of X_1 and X_2 when we know the height and waist size in inches of the person whose weight we want to predict, as we continue to follow the example given above.

When we are using multiple regression, we want to perform the process as efficiently and effectively as possible. In order to do this, we should work with the fewest number of predictor variables that allow us to develop the best prediction. The term that describes this efficiency is *parsimony*. To achieve parsimony, we must use only those predictor variables that have a fairly strong relationship to the outcome and only a weak or moderate relationship (effect) on each other. In other words, all of our predictor variables (X) must have a relationship to Y, but because they have a relationship to Y, they also have a certain level of relationship to each other (like first and second cousins and so on). What this means is that the predictor variable X_1 may be explaining part of the variation in Y that is also being explained by X_2. While we will have some overlapping of prediction by the X variables, we do not want too much as it is not efficient or effective. This overlapping of predictive ability is often referred to as *redundancy*.

When we select predictor variables, we are trying to find X values that not only have a limited amount of redundancy but that also explain different parts of the variation of Y. After all, there is no sense in making ourselves, or the persons collecting data for us, do more work than necessary. There are a number of ways we can determine which of the predictor variables are more valuable in the sense that they make a greater contribution to the efficiency and effectiveness of our prediction. One of the methods of selection that we might choose to use is referred to as *partial correlation*.

Partial correlation is the correlation (or strength of the relationship) between one predictor variable and the criterion (the Y variable in our sample) when we have removed the effect of the other predictor variable(s). In other words, we are taking care of the overlap and are only looking at the true contribution of that one particular predictor variable in explaining the variation in Y.

While the actual equation appears to be complicated, the process is really pretty easy to understand if we think in terms of correlations and use our example of height and waist size being predictors of weight. If we enter (in the following order) the height, waist size, and weight of those persons in our sample into an Excel spreadsheet I (or SPSS or other program you may wish to use), and then click on data analysis, then on correlation, the computer will do the work for us.

Figure 8.1 · Partial Correlation Example

Subject	Height (in inches)	Waist Size (in inches)	Weight (in pounds)
1	72	36	198
2	75	37	220
3	68	34	180
4	65	30	155
5	70	34	175
6	70	35	180
7	71	35	175
8	69	34	175
9	68	33	160
10	63	29	145

	Height	Waist Size	Weight
Height	1		
Waist Size	0.968545	1	
Weight	0.932885	0.905474	1

$$\frac{0.933 - (0.906)\,(0.969)}{\sqrt{1 - (0.906)^2}\;\sqrt{1 - (0.969)^2}}$$

Doing the above math (which I rounded from the correlation data; as an example, 0.932885 as the correlation between height and weight (above) rounds to 0.933) provides the following:

$$\frac{0.055}{(0.423)\,(0.247)}$$

When working the bottom portion of our math problem (directly above), remember to work the information under the two square root signs separately. As an example, in the first portion of the lower data, we would first square 0.906 and get 0.821 (rounded up). Next, we would subtract 0.821 from 1, and then find the square root, which give us 0.423. Then, continuing with the math, we would get:

$$\frac{0.055}{0.105}$$

Or, 0.524, as a measure of the influence of height on weight while controlling for waist size.

Next we repeat the process with the second combination of variables, waist size and weight:

$$\frac{0.906-(0.933)\,(0.969)}{\sqrt{1-(0.933)^2}\ \ \sqrt{1-(0.969)^2}}$$

$$\frac{0.002}{(0.359)\,(0.247)}$$

$$\frac{0.002}{0.089}$$

Or, 0.023, as a measure of the influence of waist size on weight while controlling for height.

Now we are able to see just which of the two predictor variables does the best job in helping us to predict the weight of a new subject (height does the best job at 0.524, as compared to waist size at 0.0230). The larger partial correlation is explaining more of the variation in Y. Remember, we are only looking at the size of the result of the partial correlation, not whether it is a positive or a negative number. The sign simply tells us whether the relationship is positive (both are moving in the same direction) or inverse (when one goes up the other goes down). The magnitude of the partial correlation tells us the strength of the relationship, just like when we were working with Pearson—the higher the partial correlation the better the ability to explain the variation.

We will assume that we have performed our partial correlations, and height and waist size turned out to be the best predictors of weight (keeping in mind we want to use the perfect number of predictor variable, not too many and not too few, to get the best prediction—*parsimony*). In this example, to keep things simple, we have only used two predictor variables to begin with. In reality, perhaps we would use several: height, waist size, gender, age, race, etc. In this case, we would perform our partial correlation exercise to find the very best predictors. (There is a way to do this using your computer and P values, which saves you a great many mathematical calculations, but we will get to this later.)

Generally, in multiple regression, we will let the computer do the work for us in developing our regression constants. All that we will have to do is plug in the new X values. The computer will even assist us in determining which of the X values from our sample we may wish to remove from the equation before we use the regression constants for our prediction. Since most of us have Excel on our computer, we will speak to that program.

Once you have your predictor variables (all that you have chosen to use to begin with, and that might be several) entered into your spreadsheet, you (we will use the example spreadsheet on predicting weight using height and waist size from above) click on data analysis and then on regression (note that you do not have a choice of multiple regression with this program). Once your window is open, it will ask you to identify the value you want to predict (Y) and the values you will be using to make the prediction (X). To enter the Y value, click and hold at the top of the column, which contains the value you wish to predict (weight in our example), and drag the cursor to the bottom of the data. Remember, if you have labeled the value at the top of the column with the word "weight," and you have included this label, you need to check the label box in the window (which is a good idea if you have very many variables as it will help you read the result of the computation when it prints out). Now you need to enter the X values, so you will want to make sure that the cursor is first blinking in the box for the X value location in the widow. Then click and hold the left button of the mouse at the upper corner of the X columns and drag the cursor over and down so that you encapsulate all of the X data. If you included a label with your Y data, you should capture the labels of the X data also, but since you have already clicked on the label box in the window with the Y value, you do not need to do this again.

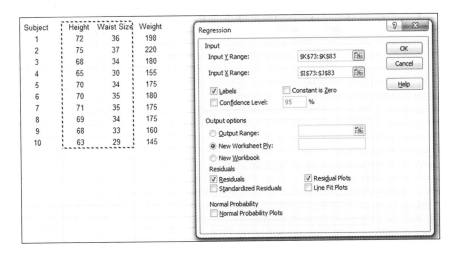

Now, click on "okay," and the computer will present your regression. To determine which variables are the better predictors, you may look at either the "P-value" column or the "t stat" column on the regression printout. Since we generally look to an alpha level of 0.05 to claim significance, you are looking for predictor variables with a "P-value" of 0.05 or lower, with numbers below 0.05 being the better predictors (0.035 as an example). You could then run the regression without the predictor(s) that has a "P-value" above 0.05 and see what happens. You may have to repeat this process more than once. Perhaps you should only remove the worst predictor, run the regression again, remove the new worst predictor, run the regression again, and so on, until you feel you have achieved parsimony. You will now have the best predictive regression constants.

If you are using the "t stat" information, you are looking for values of at least 1. Remove the X variable with the "t stat" most below the number one (1). Run the regression again and remove the X variable that now has the "t stat" most below the number one (1). You continue this process until you have the best predictor, known as achieving parsimony. Now, using the "P-value" or the "t-stat," you have the best regression constants to make a prediction with. See Figure 8.2.

Figure 8.2

Summary Output

Regression Statistics	
Multiple R	0.932918
R Square	0.870336
Adjusted R Square	0.833289
Standard Error	8.727569
Observations	10

ANOVA

	df	SS	MS	F	Significance F
Regression	2	3,578.907	1,789.453	23.49275	0.000785
Residual	7	533.1932	76.17046		
Total	9	4,112.1			

	Coefficients	Standard Error	t Stat	P-value	Lower 95.0%	Upper 95.0%	Lower 95.0%	Upper 95.0%
Intercept	−223.225	92.57188	−2.41137	0.04668	−442.123	−4.32732	−442.123	−4.32732
Height	5.651482	3.424408	1.650353	0.142856	−2.44596	13.74892	−2.44596	13.74892
Waist Size	0.267289	4.682652	0.057081	0.956076	−10.8054	11.34	−10.8054	11.34

Notice in our example of a regression printout from Excel (directly above), that the lowest (thus the best) P-value is the value associated with the height of the individual (P-value of 0.142856) as compared to the waist size (0.956076).

This information corresponds with the highest t stat (1.650353 for height and 0.057081 for waist size). We only have two predictor variables in our example, so we would not want to throw either out. However, if we were using several, we would do some "weeding" to come to *parsimony*.

Once we have selected the best predictor variables (X), we are ready to work our regression and predict the weight of a new subject. As an example, let's predict the weight of someone who is 5'8" (68") and has a waist of 33".

As you remember, the equation is:

$$\tilde{Y} = b_1 x_1 + b_2 x_2 + a$$

To work the formula, we simply go up to our printout of the multiple regression and grab the data we need: b is the slope (coefficient) for height, or 5.652 (rounded); X is the new value for height we will use to make our prediction; b is the coefficient for waist size, or 0.267 (rounded); and X is the new value for waist size we will apply to our prediction. The letter "a" represents the intercept, or −223.225.

Plugging all of this is we have:

$$\tilde{Y} = 5.652\ (68) + 0.267\ (33) + -223.225$$
$$= 384.34 + 8.81 - 223.23$$
$$= 169.92, \text{ or } 170 \text{ pounds}$$

There are a few other points we should note while we are working with multiple regression and our Excel printout (or any other program you might be using). First, as you look at the Excel printout above, note that at the upper left corner you will find a great deal of useful information. The *standard error* is one of these useful bits of data. In this case, the *standard error* is noted at 8.728 (rounded). If we wanted to feel 95% confident that we had captured the predicted weight of someone who is 5'8" tall (68") and had a waist of 33", we would take our *standard error* and multiply it by 1.96 (which is the z score for 95%). Thus, we would have 170 plus and minus 17.11 (rounded), or we would predict that someone who was 5'8" tall and had a waist of 33" would weigh between 163 and 187 pounds.

There are some other terms and values with which we need to be concerned as we look at the printout of our multiple regression. Like some of the previous vocabulary, these terms can be a bit unnerving, but we will cover them one-by-one. They are *multicollinearity, multiple correlation coefficient, standard error of the estimate* and *shrinkage*.

The first term we need to familiarize ourselves with is *multicollinearity*. Multicollinearity refers to the amount of correlation that occurs between the various predictor variables. Remember, while we are likely to have some intercorrelation, we do not want too much as it makes it more difficult to arrive at an efficient and effective regression solution. Generally speaking, we would prefer to have correlations between our various predictor variables of no higher than 0.80 (you may have noticed that we used correlations to develop the partial correlations we worked on above). When you run the correlations between your predictor variables and find, as an example, two of them are correlated with each other at 0.87, you would chose to drop one of the highly correlated variables from your equation. What we are doing is eliminating as much redundancy as possible, the same purpose of partial correlation, so that we have the most efficient prediction possible (parsimony). Of course, the very best situation would be to have several predictor variables, all of which are related to the Y variable but have absolutely no relationship with each other, which is not likely to happen.

The *multiple correlation coefficient* works the same as the correlation coefficient (Pearson's r) that you are already familiar with and will show on your Excel printout as Multiple R. If you square the Multiple R (*Multiple Coefficient of Determination*), you will know the percentage of the question (change) of the Y variable that is answered by your predictor variables (and conversely, the percentage of change in the Y variable that is not accounted for by the predictor variables).

The *standard error of estimate* allows us to make predictions with a given specification of accuracy and is computed automatically as one standard error (which is used very much like one standard deviation). As an example, if (changing our numbers a little for fun) using multiple regression we predicted the weight of someone who was 5'8" and had a waist size of 33" to be 160 pounds, we would know intuitively that not everyone who was 5'8" and had a waist of 33" would weigh 160 pounds as we always have to deal with error. If our printout indicated we had a standard error of 10 pounds, we could then say we would predict with 68% confidence (accuracy) that someone who was 5'8" and had a waist of 33" would weigh somewhere between 150 and 170 pounds (and being right a little better than two out of three times is not bad). If we wanted to be 95% confident, we would multiply the standard error by 1.96, which is developed from the z-score for an alpha of 0.05 (rather than multiplying by two as we would with standard deviations) and state that a person who was 5'8" and had a waist of 33" would weigh between 140 (140.4) and 179 (179.6) pounds.

The last regression term we will be concerned about in this text is *shrinkage*. We developed our regression on how height and waist size affects weight using a very specific sample of people. If we try to transfer this regression to another group of people (or an individual) that is different in any way from the original sample, we will lose some of the predictive ability of our original regression (R^2) as it relates to the percentage of change in Y that is explained by the X variables. Adjusted R^2 therefore makes a correction to allow for the additional probable error when we make predictions for units not part of our original sample. As an example, we may have a Multiple R of 0.93, a R-squared of 0.87, and an Adjusted R-squared of 0.83.

Chapter Nine

Hypothesis Testing and The t Test

The *Student's t Test* permits us to determine whether an apparent difference between two groups is large enough to be statistically significant. As you remember, in hypothesis testing we develop a null hypothesis (H_0), which presents the observed differences between two variables or groups as insignificant. The alternative hypothesis (H_1 or H_A) claims that any difference we are observing is statistically significant. In other words, it is not occurring by pure chance, but is real and caused by some outside influence. When we test the hypothesis, we are determining the probability that the null hypothesis is indeed true. Generally, we set this test at an alpha of 0.05. This means that out of 100 samples, we would only get this result by pure chance 5 times; the other 95 times something is causing the outcome we are observing.

The t test, like the z test, is based upon the z distribution, or the standard normal curve (bell curve). As you remember, the mean for the sample is located right in the middle, or high point, of the bell curve. As we move to the right (positive) or the left (negative) of the mean, we gradually encompass more and more of our data points on a diminishing scale (more of the points will be clustered toward the mean and the further away we move from the mean in a normal distribution the fewer data points there should be). By moving to both the right and left of the mean at one standard deviation, we will encompass 68% of our data points. If we go out to two standard deviations, both to the right and left of the mean, we will encompass 95% of the data points, and if we go on out to three standard deviations in both directions, we will have captured almost all of the data points (99.74%).

It would then stand to reason that the further away we get from the mean, either in the positive (right) or negative (left) direction, the less likely we are to find a data point. Therefore, if we go out two standard deviations (z score of 1.96) or more from the mean in either direction, a data point would only have a 5% chance of occurring (2.5% if we are considering only the positive or negative side of the curve). This is not much of a chance of random occurrence, so a point occurring at or beyond two standard deviations would be statistically significant in our testing.

How the Z Score Fits In

We can make good use of this knowledge if we want to compare an individual with a group to determine if that individual has exceeded expectations enough to either be rewarded or disciplined, depending upon whether they excel on the positive or negative side of the curve. As an example, if we wanted to reward someone for production, we would look for z scores that would be +1.96 or higher. If we wanted to study absenteeism and identify those individuals who were perhaps in need of some type of counseling or motivation, we would again look for people with z scores of +1.96 or higher (because, if we are counting sick days used, these would be the people who were using far more sick days, when we hold shifts or other influencing circumstances in check). As an example, if we were concerned with the usage of sick time, we would want to develop an average of sick time taken during the period under consideration for each of the three shifts we are running (if we are running three shifts). We do this because conditions are different on each shift and those varied conditions might influence the number of sick days used. We then develop the z score based upon a comparison with the mean number of sick days taken by persons on that shift. We would do the same thing for production, as there might be shift conditions that influence output. Once we have the z score though, we can make comparisons with everyone on the department, as z scores give us the ability to compare things that are otherwise not truly comparable, like apples and oranges as the old saying goes.

As an example, let's work the equation we would use to develop an individual z score.

$$Z = \frac{X - \overline{X}}{S}$$

This equation tells us that in order to find the z score for an individual, we subtract the group mean from the individual score and then divide by the standard deviation for the group. As an example, if the individual had taken 17 sick days this past year, the group mean for the shift was 13 sick days for the year, and the standard deviation for the shift was 1.8, the individual z score for the officer is 17 − 13 / 1.8 = 2.222. The z score, when we look at the z table (found in the back of this text), for this officer is beyond 1.96. So we would want to investigate the cause of the excessive absenteeism.

To move from the comparison of individuals to the comparison of groups, we need to slightly adjust our techniques and thinking. When we have a distribution of data (frequency distributions), it is possible to present the information in the terms of summary statistics, such as *mean, median, and standard deviation*. The term that is used in statistics, when we present frequency distributions in the form of summary statistics, is *sampling distributions*. It is important to remember at this point that we construct our sampling distributions from a population. As an example, when we worked the z score problem above, we were comparing an individual's use of sick days with the average number of sick days used by everyone on the shift (thus the population of the shift). Without going into a great deal of detail on the development of a sampling distribution, we do need to introduce another term: *sampling with replacement*.

Sampling with Replacement

Sampling with replacement is a technique wherein a sample is drawn from a large population and the mean is computed for that sample. The sample is then returned to the population, and another sample is drawn. The mean is computed for the second sample and then the sample is returned to the population. A third sample is drawn, and so on, until a large number of samples have been drawn and their means assembled into a frequency distribution, just like raw scores. This distribution of the means of the drawn samples is referred to as our next new term: a *sampling distribution of the mean*.

Sampling Distribution of the Mean

The sampling distribution of the mean is useful when we want to compare a sample of individuals (rather than an individual), which we hypothesize is not statistically different from a population on a given characteristic (say sick time taken, job satisfaction ratings, or even exam scores).

As an example, let's say that a university offers a bachelor of criminal justice degree and requires graduating seniors to take a standardized exam as part of an outcome assessment program for the university. Rather than taking the time and expense to test all graduating seniors in the criminal justice program, the following year the university decides to test a randomly selected sample of graduating criminal justice seniors. After administering the exam to the sample, the university develops the null hypothesis that: The mean exam score of

93 of the sample with an N of 43 is not statistically significantly different from the population of students whose mean exam score was 96. Of course, the alternative hypothesis would then be: The mean exam score of 93 of the sample is statistically different from the population of students whose mean exam score was 96. The standard deviation is 10.4.

Application of the following equation permits us to test our hypothesis:

$$z = \frac{\bar{x} - \mu}{\sigma_{\bar{x}}} = \frac{\bar{x} - \mu}{(\sigma/\sqrt{n})}$$

Of course we have to allow for error that will occur with the use of a sample. We do this by combining the equation for the *standard error of the mean* with the equation that compares the z score values of the sample and the population. We use z score values when the sample is large enough (30 or more). We will apply the standard of 0.05 to determine if a test reveals a difference that is significant. Since we are using z score values, we simply compare the result of our test to the z score value of 1.96. We are using 1.96 as the critical value because this is the point where we account for 95% of the value of the sample means drawn from the population.

As an example, continuing with the example from above, we would first develop our null and alternative hypothesis.

H_0: Graduating students whose mean exam score was 93 are not different from the population of students whose mean exam score was 96.

H_1: Graduating students whose mean exam score was 93 are different from the population of students whose mean exam score was 96.

We are now at the next-to-the-last chapter in the text, and you should be feeling pretty good about reading formulas. Look at the above formula for testing the hypothesis, plug in the numbers, and give it a go!

Based upon our test, and using 1.96 as the critical score and 10.4 as the standard deviation, we see that we would reject our null hypothesis. Remember, we can do this if we can consider our sampling distribution of the mean to be normal. We consider our distribution normal if the population is normal and we have a large enough sample size, generally 30 or more. While we may be concerned with the normalcy of our population, we may proceed if our sample is large enough (at least 30) because of the *central limits theorem*.

In the above problem our processed math would look like this:

$$93 - 96 = -3 \qquad 10.4 / 6.56 = 1.59 \qquad -3 / 1.59 = 1.89$$

Since 1.89 is less than 1.96, we did not find significance, and we would fail to reject the null hypothesis and conclude that, with the information available at the time of the test, the scores of the population of the graduate students in the exam were not significantly different from the scores of the graduate students in the sample.

The Central Limits Theorem

Generally, the *central limits theorem* holds that, regardless of the shape of the population, the sample will develop a normal distribution upon a proper drawing (a random drawing) of the sample. Of course, the central limits theorem applies only if the shape of the population is not normal, as there is no need for the theorem if the population has a normal distribution (shaped like a bell curve). The size of our sample will make the adaptation to a normal shape based upon the size of the sample and how abnormal the distribution of our population happens to be. If the distribution of the population is not very abnormal, we will be able to work with a smaller sample. If the distribution of the population is quite abnormal, we will need a larger sample to make the correction toward normalcy.

However, it is possible that we will have a population that is abnormal in its distribution, but, at the same time, we are not in a position to obtain a sample of sufficient number to account for the abnormality of the population. In this case, we use a testing procedure that is referred to as a *t distribution* (commonly referred to as Student's t distribution).

$$t = \frac{\bar{x} - \mu}{\frac{s}{\sqrt{N}}}$$

You may have noticed that this equation is the same as the equation for calculating the z score value. The process is different from the z score testing method, as we cannot simply use 1.96 as the critical value for an alpha of 0.05.

Rather, we must consult a table that will provide the critical value based upon the size of our sample. We apply the t testing method when our sample is generally smaller than 30. However, you may use the t test with any size sample, as the table converts to the z value standard once we reach a sample size of 30. The t test is also used when the standard deviation of the population is unknown (which may often be the case). We do this by substituting the population standard deviation (σ) with the sample standard deviation (s).

Degrees of Freedom

Finding the critical value of the t is fairly simple; all we need to know is the alpha level we wish to apply (generally 0.05) and the degrees of freedom. The degrees of freedom is computed by taking the "N" of the sample (how many people are in our sample) and subtracting one (1) or ($N - 1$). As an example, if we have a sample with an "N" of 19, we would have 18 degrees of freedom. When we consult the table, we would find the intersection of 18 degrees of freedom and an alpha of 0.05, which provides a critical value of 2.101 for a two-tailed test. The "t" we compute will need to be as large as, or larger than, 2.101 for us to claim our test is significant and "reject the null hypothesis." We set up our test following the same method we used for the previous example on z score values.

Non-Directional and Directional Testing

While discussing t testing above, you should have noticed *two-tailed* testing being mentioned. We may perform our tests in either a one-tailed or a two-tailed manner, depending upon whether we are able to anticipate a direction of movement with our test. Our decision to apply a one-tailed or two-tailed test will determine how we phrase our hypothesis and the level of the critical value we use to determine significance.

If we wish to know whether the mean of our sample is significantly "more or less," we would apply a non-directional (or two-tailed) test. In other words, we just want to know if there is enough of a difference between our sample mean and the population mean to be significant. We really do not care if that movement is to the positive side or the negative side of the population mean. However, if we can anticipate the direction of the movement, to the positive side of the population mean for instance, and we really do not care about the significance of any movement to the negative side of the population mean, we would use a one-tailed test.

You, as the author of the test, will make the decision as to whether to use a one-tailed or two-tailed test. In doing so, you will want to consider that (1) you can always choose to perform a two-tailed test, whether you can anticipate the direction of movement or not, and (2) the critical value required to claim significance will be higher if you run a two-tailed test. This means that it will be more difficult to claim significance if you choose to use a two-tailed test. On the other hand, while choosing to run the two-tailed test may make it more difficult for you to claim significance, it also makes your finding more valuable. As an example, in trying to jump over a bar extended between two poles at a height of three (3) feet above the ground, some people would be impressed to clear the bar without knocking it away from the two supporting poles. On the other hand, if that bar is set four (4) feet above the ground, an ability to clear the bar would be much more impressive. The bar set three feet above the ground would be the one-tailed test. The bar set four feet above the ground is the two-tailed test. Generally, it is better to run a two-tailed test in all situations.

Independent and Related Samples

When comparing two samples, we must consider whether the samples are independent in nature, or whether they are related (or paired) samples. If the two samples are independent of each other (have no connection or relationship), we would use the following equation to test whether there is a significant difference between our measurement of samples one and two.

$$t = \frac{\overline{X}_1 - \overline{X}_2}{\sqrt{\left[\dfrac{1}{N_1} + \dfrac{1}{N_2}\right]\left[\dfrac{s_1^2(N_1 - 1) + s_2^2(N_2 - 1)}{N_1 + N_2 - 2}\right]}}$$

You will notice that we are performing a t test as compared to a z score test. There is a z score test that will make this comparison, but since a t test may be used regardless of the sample size, and a z score test must have a sample of 30 or larger, we will only review the t test in this text. Of course, to use the t test for an independent sample we are making several assumptions: (a) the samples were drawn independently and in a random manner; (b) the samples are mutually exclusive of each other; (c) the populations from which we randomly selected our samples are of a uniform structure or composition; and (d) the sampling distribution is normal in nature.

Working the equation is relatively simple if we undertake the process in sections. First, looking above the horizontal line of the equation, we notice that we are subtracting the mean of Sample 2 from the mean of Sample 1. As an example, if the mean of Sample 1 is 27 (the class average in a criminology course, out of 30 total possible points, using teaching method "A") and the mean of Sample 2 is 22 (the class average in a criminology course, out of 30 total possible points, using teaching method "B"), we would have $27 - 22 = 5$. Once we have completed this step, we can now consider the portion of the equation found below the horizontal line.

The first thing we should notice and be sure not to forget is that once we have completed the math, we must go to the square root. Forgetting to do so is a common mistake for students and will make your answer very, very wrong.

Looking at the lower portion of the equation, you will notice there are really two portions to the equation, with each portion enclosed in brackets. You work each bracket separately, and then work the results in a final step. The first bracket tells us to divide the number one (1) by the N (how many elements) of Sample 1 and then add that result to the number one (1) divided by the N of Sample 2. As an example, if Sample 1 had an N of 8, and Sample 2 had an N of 6 we would have $1/8 + 1/6 = 0.292$. Put the result of your computations into the first bracket, where the first portion of the equation was.

Now, move to the second bracket. While this looks more complicated, it is really fairly easy to perform. Look at the top portion of the equation first. We are told to take the variance (note the equation is calling for the variance, not the standard deviation) of Sample 1 and to multiply that variance by the N of Sample 1, minus 1. We would add the result of this calculation to the result of the variance of Sample 2 times the N of Sample 2 minus 1. As an example, if the variance of Sample 1 is 3 and the N of sample 1 is 8; the variance of Sample 2 is 4 and the size of Sample 2 is 6, we would perform the following calculation: $3(7) + 4(5) = 41$.

Now we move to the lower portion of this section of the equation. Here we find that we are told to take the N of Sample 1, add it to the N of Sample 2, and then subtract 2. As an example, continuing from the above paragraph, we would have $8 + 6 = 14 - 2 = 12$. Now divide 41 by 12 to get 3.42.

There is one last step need to complete the lower portion of this section of the equation. We now (taking our results from the above two paragraphs) multiply 0.292 by $3.42 = 0.999$. Next, and this is what students often forget to do, hit the square root key of your calculator to get 0.9994998, or 1.0 if we round.

To complete our calculation, we take the result of the calculation performed above the horizontal line and divide by the result of the calculation performed below the horizontal line. As an example (drawing from above), we would have 5 divided by 1 = 5.

Of course, with all hypothesis testing, we would have previously developed a null and alternative hypothesis concerning the two samples. Now that we have performed our test, we must determine if the results are significant so we would know whether we should "reject" or "fail to reject" the null hypothesis. To make this determination, we need to find the degrees of freedom. To find the degree of freedom for a t test of independent samples, we take the N of Sample 1, and the N of Sample 2, and then subtract 2. As an example (continuing our work from the above paragraphs), we would have 8 + 6 = 14 − 2 = 12. We have 12 degrees of freedom, and if we test at the 0.05 level (two-tailed test), we would find, upon consulting our table, the critical value is 2.179. We would then compare our calculated t of 5 to the critical value of 2.179. Our calculated value is as large as or larger than the critical value, so, we would "reject" the null hypothesis. As an example, if our null hypothesis was that "the outcome of the criminology instruction methods do not differ," and the alternative hypothesis was that "the outcome of the criminology instruction methods do differ," we would, with the data available to us at the time of the study, reject the null hypothesis. The outcome of the criminology instruction methods do appear to differ.

Keep in mind that we have performed a two-tailed test, so we are looking for a significant difference in either direction. Since we are looking for significance in either direction (positive or negative), a calculated t value of -5 would be just as significant as a calculated t value of +5. Looking at our mean averaged test scores, we are concerned with the outcome of criminological instruction methods, and we have chosen the final point average of the two samples as a means of comparison. Our test has indicated that the method of instruction for the population from which Sample 1 was drawn (Sample 1 had the higher mean point score) is the better method of instruction for this course in criminology.

It is possible when we are performing a study that our samples may be related (paired) to each other in some manner. This may occur if we are collecting data from the same sample, or group, at two different time periods (say the start and end of a semester). A relationship might also develop if the people in the sample spend a great deal of time together—a married couple for instance, or perhaps two police officers who have worked as a patrol team for a period of time. When we have a related sample, we apply a different equation:

$$t = \frac{\Sigma d}{\sqrt{\dfrac{N\Sigma d^2 - (\Sigma d)^2}{N-1}}}$$

Looking above the horizontal line, we see that we are told to sum the differences. As an example, if we pulled a sample of 20 husbands and wives, and we wanted to determine if there was a significant difference in how they (the men as compared to the women) viewed the level of violence in the media, we might have them separately rank the level of violence from 1 (little violence) to 4 (very violent), with 2 and 3 being somewhere between the two extremes. We would then compare each pair to see what the difference in their impression of the level of violence in the media is. For instance, if the male member of the pair ranked the level of violence at 2, and the female of the pair ranked the level of the violence at 4, the difference would be 2. We would do this for every pair and then sum the differences.

Looking below the horizontal line, we once again see that after the computations, we must go to the square root. Under the square root sign, we see a horizontal line with the equation above the horizontal line giving us specific instructions. We are told to take the N of the sample and multiply the N by the sum of the squared differences. As an example, if we had a difference for couple #1 of 2, the square for this couple would be 4. We would square the difference of every couple and then sum all of the squared differences, and this is what we would multiply by N. From the result of this calculation we would then subtract the sum of the differences squared. As an example, if the difference for couple #1 was 2, the difference for couple #2 was 1, the difference for couple #3 was 3, and so on, we would add 2 + 1 + 3, etc. Once we had summed all the differences we would then square the summed difference. Therefore, if our summed differences was 27 we would square 27 to get 729, and that is what we would plug into this part of the equation.

Now, it is time to move to the portion of the equation that is below the horizontal line. This portion is quite simple, the N of the sample minus one (1).

As an example, if we had a sample of 6 pairs, let's say husband and wife, and we were concerned about the fear of terror following the 9/11 attack in New York. We would first develop a null and alternative hypothesis: The level of fear felt by men and women does not differ; the level of fear felt by men and women does differ. We would then circulate our study (greatly simplified for

Pair #	Husband	Wife	Difference	Difference squared
1	3	2	1	1
2	2	2	0	0
3	3	1	2	4
4	1	1	0	0
5	2	3	1	1
6	4	2	2	4
			6	10

this example) that asks the participants to rate their level of fear using some type of scale, perhaps 1 (no feeling of fear), 2 (a slight feeling of fear), 3 (a moderate feeling of fear), and 4 (very fearful).

Plugging our data into the equation, we develop the following: Above the horizontal line, we have the sum of the difference, which is 6. Below the horizontal line, and under the square root sign, we had N (6) times the sum of the difference-squared (10) minus the sum of the difference, that we then square (36), all of which we then divide by N − 1 (6 − 1), then hit the square root key on our calculator. We now have 6 / 2.19 = 2.74.

Our next step is to consult the t-table to determine the critical value at an alpha of 0.05 and 5 degrees of freedom (df = N − 1). The critical value from the t-table is 2.571. Since we are running a two-tailed test, looking for any significant movement, it does not make any difference if our calculated t is a positive or negative number. Our calculated t is 2.739, which is slightly smaller than the critical value of 2.571, so we would *fail to reject the null hypothesis*. However, we are so close to the critical value (keep in mind we are using an ex-

tremely small sample), we would suggest that the study be conducted once
again with another sample.

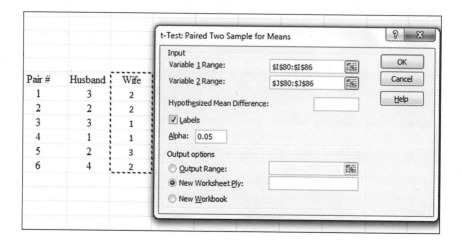

Chapter Ten

One-Way Analysis of Variance

When we perform a statistical test, we are always faced with a certain amount of error. As an example, sometimes the decisions we make in life are pretty good and other times we wish we would have spent a little more time thinking about what we were going to do. In other words, we have more error in our thinking process than we would like.

Type I and Type II Error

In statistics we talk about two types of error, Type I and Type II error, and we talk about this type of error when we are doing hypothesis testing. One type of error occurs when we reject the null hypothesis (H_0) when it is true and we call this error a Type I error. The other type of error we might make is a Type II error, and this is when we do not to reject the null hypothesis (H_0) when it is false and we should have rejected it. A Type I error is the more serious mistake to make, but fortunately we have a way to control the odds that we will mess up and make a Type I error. We do this by setting the alpha level when we do a statistical test.

As you remember from our past chapters, statistical programs default to 0.05 as the alpha level. And, as you remember, the alpha level is the number of times out of 100 samples we might expect to find that what we are interested in and observing happens purely by chance while the other 95 times something is making it happen. This is really important to keep in mind because we have one other little problem to consider, and that is every time we run a directly connected statistical test, or multiple statistical tests, we increase the chance that we will make a Type I error. We will confront this problem if we have more than two things that we want to compare against each other, as in a case where we wanted to compare the tests scores of three groups of students, with each group of students being taught using a different method. Of course, if we were only comparing two groups of student test scores and methods, we would most likely use some form of the t test. More about that in a few minutes when we talk about ANOVA (Analysis of Variance), as I think we need to spend a little more time on error.

Type I error is the most serious of the two types of error that we might make. As an example, if we were walking down the street and observed someone laying on the sidewalk, and not seeming to be breathing, a couple of things might happen. First, we might make the assumption (our alternative hypothesis (H_1)) that the person is dead and there is nothing that we could do to help him or her and we simply continue on down the street. Or, we could make the assumption (our null hypothesis (H_0)) that the person was not dead and we would try to apply CPR until help arrived.

If we reject our null hypothesis, which tells us that the person is not dead, we would go merrily on down the street without stopping to administer CPR and the person would die before other help arrived. This is called rejecting the null hypothesis when it is true (the person was not dead) and is the more serious of the two errors to make. On the other hand, if our alternative hypothesis (the person is already dead) was correct but we stopped and administered CPR anyhow, we would be committing a Type II error, which is not as serious as a Type I error. In other words, we failed to reject (throw out) the null that says that the person was not dead and in doing so we made a Type II error, and acting upon that error performed CPR on a corpse. Not necessarily a pleasant thing to do, but at least we did not stand by as a living person was lying on the sidewalk and slowly died (which was the Type I error).

Analysis of Variance (ANOVA)

Quite a few years ago now, a rather famous statistician named Sir Robert Fisher developed a method of testing multiple groups without putting us in the position of encountering a high risk of making a Type I error. This method is known as the *analysis of variance (ANOVA)*, and while it is possible to do the computations by hand it takes some time to work all of the numbers and so we will let our computer do the work for us in this particular test. What we have to keep in mind while our computer is doing the calculations is that ANOVA will test for statistical significance in the difference between all of the groups we are testing at once. In order to do this our computer, using a statistical program, will actually be looking at two different things.

First the computer will consider the *error variance*. The error variance is a naturally-occurring event that is no more than how far each individual score in that group is from the mean score of that same group. This should sound pretty familiar as we chatted about mean and variance in past chapters. Since we are, or rather our computer is, comparing this variance within each individual group at one time, we normally will refer to this as a *within-group variance*.

The second type of variance is titled as *treatment variance*. The treatment is what we are doing to the groups that might be making a difference in the outcome of the groups. As an example, teaching a course in statistical analysis to three sections of students, one section (S-1) might be required to purchase a text and at the end of nine weeks take a test about statistical analysis. At the same time, a second group of students (S-2) might not be required to purchase a text, but would only attend lecture once per week on performing statistical analysis. At the end of the ninth week, this second group of students would also take the test given to the S-1. For the third group (S-3), they would be required to purchase the text as well as attend lecture once a week. At the end of the nine weeks, all three sections would be given the test, originally given to S-1 and S-2. The question would be, whether one method of teaching statistics works better than the other. Performance of an ANOVA would help to answer the question. What the computer will be doing is to develop the treatment variance by taking the individual mean of each of the three groups of students (sections of students; S-1, S-2, and S-3) and comparing each of those means to the *Grand Mean* to find the difference (the variance). The grand mean is what we have if we take the three individual means, add them together, and then divide by three. In other words, it is the mean of the mean of the three groups of students all smoothed out into one overarching mean ... the grand mean. By the way, the grand mean is also called the *between-group variance*.

There are equations and lots of math if we want to work an ANOVA out by hand as well as additional terminology, such as the *sum of squares (SS)* and *degrees of freedom (df)* and more, but for our introduction and basic understanding we are going to jump to how we read the printout our computer is going to make for us. If you take a more-advanced class in statistics at some point in the future you will go into a greater depth of the workings of ANOVA and can have fun with the math at that time. But for now, we will make up some test scores for the three groups of students mentioned above and see what happens. See Figure 10.1 on the next page.

Figure 10.1 · Score of Test Groups of Students

(S-1)	(S-2)	(S-3)
95	93	96
92	89	94
89	85	96
92	91	94
94	92	97
95	93	95
81	83	88
86	85	89
87	89	93

The first thing we need to do is to enter our test data into an Excel spreadsheet, as we have done in past chapters. However, in this case you will have three choices to make: ANOVA: Single Factor; ANOVA: Two-Factor with Replication; ANOVA: Two-Factor without Replication. For the sake of understanding ANOVA, we will stick with the Single Factor model. Remember, if you label the columns you need to check the little block when you come to that point in the analysis and let the computer know you are using column labels. Then click on "OK" and the program will perform the calculations for us. One other thing, please note, the program will ask us if the data is in columns or rows, and you will need to check the proper designation or the computer will not work the problem properly.

Once we have the computer do the work for us using the above data we will have a return that looks like Figure 10.2.

Figure 10.2

ANOVA: Single Factor

SUMMARY

Groups	Count	Sum	Average	Variance
(S-1)	9	811	90.11111	22.61111
(S-2)	9	800	88.88889	14.11111
(S-3)	9	849	94.33333	10.5

ANOVA

Source of Variation	SS	df	MS	F	P-value	F crit
Between Groups	146.8889	2	73.44444	4.665882	0.019419	3.402826
Within Groups	377.7778	24	15.74074			
Total	524.6667	2				

Looking at Figure 10.2, we can see that the program used 26 degrees of freedom in the computation, and this number was developed by summing the 2 degrees of freedom (*df*) Between Groups and the 24 degrees of freedom Within Groups. We found these degrees of freedom by taking the three groups and subtracting one group (3 − 1 = 2 *df*) and the 27 degrees of freedom within the groups (9 X 3 = 27 −3 = 24) and then adding 24 + 2 to have 26 degrees of freedom in our calculations. But how do we know if we have a significant finding in our ANOVA?

Look at the F (4.665882) and the F crit (3.402826), and notice that the F is larger than the F crit (crit means the critical value). If the F is as large as, or larger than, the F crit, we know we have a significant finding and that one method of instructing seems to be superior. We should also look at the P-value

(0.019419), and if it is 0.05 or less, we have a confirmation that we have a significant finding. In this case, the P-value is quite a bit smaller than 0.05 and, at 2 chances (0.019419, or 0.02 rounded) that what we are observing would happen out of 100 samples, we have a very significant finding to report. We know which instructional method is best by looking at the average score and noting that S-3 has the larger average score, and with a significant finding we would recommend that we use the combination of a text and lecture to return the best results on the learning of the students.

In our example, a null hypothesis might have been developed, proposing there is no significant difference in test scores based upon the three methods of instruction. The alternative hypothesis would have proposed that the test scores would be significantly affected by the method of instruction.

H_0: Examination scores are not significantly affected by the method of instruction.

H_1: Examination scores are significantly affected by the method of instruction.

In the case of our example, we did have a significant finding, and so we would state, "With the data available to us at the time of the statistical testing, we did find a significant difference in exam scores between the three groups of students and reject the null hypothesis." Based upon the analysis of our ANOVA, the group of students who were exposed to a combined lecture and text format did, as a group, significantly better on the exam (or at least we think so, at this point).

There is one last point concerning ANOVA, given this is a course in basic statistical analysis. Before we apply ANOVA, we need to make sure that we have met four very basic assumptions: 1) all of our groups were drawn by random sample from the population under study; 2) our groups are independent in that no person is a member of more than one of the groups; 3) the population variances from which the groups are constructed are homogeneous; and 4) the variable that we are interested in is normally distributed across the population of interest from which our sample is drawn.

Level of Significance and the Decision Rule

When we use our computer and a statistical program, the printout will provide the F-value and the F-crit for us to compare. But we would need to write our hypothesis a little differently because of a number of possible outcomes in our test. We need to make the rival hypothesis (the alternative hypothesis,

H_1) all-inclusive. In order to accomplish this, we would write our alternative hypothesis simply as H_1 = Not H_0. As an example, from our exercise on teaching methods and student outcomes we might write our hypothesis like this:

H_0: The teaching method applied would not cause a significant difference in the final scores of the students enrolled in the course, or H_0: $S_1 = S_2 = S_3$

H_1: Not H_0

If we work our ANOVA by hand, once we had computed the value of F, we would need to consult an ANOVA table to find the F-crit. Computation of ANOVA by hand is possible, and it can be done that way, but it is a great deal of work for an introductory class. So we will not really practice the by-hand method. For our purpose, it is enough to see how the table would be used to find the critical value (F-crit). When we look at the table, we would find the between-group difference across the top of the table and the within-group difference along the side of the table. We then must decide the alpha level we wish to use, and remembering that 0.05 is the default for most situations, we decide to use the 0.05 table find where the two *df* would come together in the table, tracking the between-group line down and the within-group line across, until they intersect. This point is where we find the F-crit listed.

ANOVA is a one-tailed test because we expect that the numerator will be equal to or larger than the denominator. What this means to us is that we compare the F-value to the F-crit and, in order to reject the null hypothesis, our F must be as large as, or larger than, the F-crit. When we use a program to do the work for us, our printout will also show us the P-value of our ANOVA and, as we know, we are looking for a P-value of 0.05 or smaller in order to reject the null hypothesis.

Once we have found that we have a significant difference (and we have rejected the null hypothesis that there is no statistically-significant difference), we are faced with a new problem. We have a difference, but how do we know which of the treatments (in our example, the treatments are the three different methods of instruction) is the treatment that is causing the significance?

Post Hoc Testing

In order to help us, processes known as *post hoc tests* were developed by various statisticians over a period of several decades. A post hoc ("post" = after) test is performed after the ANOVA and will tell us whether we have a significant finding or not. If we do not have a significant finding with our ANOVA, there is no need to run a post hoc test. While there are a variety of post hoc tests, our purpose in this text is best served to look at one that can be used in most situations. The test was developed by a statistician named John W. Tukey and is known as the *Tukey Honestly Significant Difference (HSD)*. The test works for us because it cuts down on the possibility of a Type I error at the point of the alpha level, no matter how many groups we might happen to be comparing. As an example, rather than testing three testing methods by using three groups of students, we might have five teaching methods and use five groups of students in our experiment.

Briefly, as this is a basic text, the HSD works by computing the *absolute difference of all pairs of means*. Once this has been done, one finds what is termed the *q value*. There are a number of steps that one would go through to include finding the *harmonic mean of the group*. All of this is beyond the work typically found in a basic text on statistical analysis, but it is beneficial to become exposed to the terminology, in any case.

What is important with respect to the level of statistics covered in this text is that we need to keep in mind that *statistical significance* is really the probability of our making a *Type 1* error. If our computed F is as large as, or larger than, the F crit, we are able to say that our results are significant beyond the 0.05 level and that the probability that we have made a *Type 1* error is less than 5%.

We do face one other problem with ANOVA and the F value (sometimes called the F ratio). Just because we have a significant finding does not mean that it will be easy to decide which treatment is effective to a greater extent than any other of the tested treatments. In our example, S-3 (an average of 94.33333) was obviously more influential than the other treatments tested, but this will not always be the case. If the mean scores (94.33333, 90.11111, and 88.88889 in our example) are only a point or two apart, we have a problem.

There is a fairly straight-forward method to check on how useful our just-completed calculations are, and that is by working η^2 (which is the lower-case Greek eta squared). The information we need to perform this calculation is found in our ANOVA summary table as seen in Figure 10.2. The formula we would use is:

$$\eta^2 = \frac{SS_{bg}}{SS_{total}}$$

The formula is actually easy, as it is asking us to take the *sum of squares between groups* and divide that number by the *sum of squares total*. From our data above (Figure 10.2) we would find η^2 by taking 146.8889 and dividing that number by 524.6667 and coming up with an η^2 of 0.2799661, which we could round to 0.28. This is pretty low, and tells us that 28% of the variance in the test scores is caused by the instructional methods used on the three groups of students. We can go one step further and go to the square root of η^2 and come up with 0.5291182, which we could then round to 53%, which is the correlation between the test scores and our instructional methods. Knowing that 53% of the result of the test scores was caused by the instructional methods, and that what was apparently the best instructional method was used on student group S-3, future classes could be prepared with the combination of text and lecture.

For a little more practice on ANOVA, see the Chapter Exercises at the end of this text.

Chapter Exercises

The purpose of this set of exercises is to provide practice to the student as he or she familiarizes himself or herself with the process of the particular statistical method applied in that chapter. It is not necessary to provide large numbers of exercises as the process is the same, and it is a simple matter to self-create additional exercises if the student so desires.

If you do not remember how to perform the following exercises, simply return to the appropriate chapter and review the process of how perform the calculation or how to enter the data into Excel.

Note: There are no exercises for Chapter 4.

Chapter One

Mean, Median, and Mode

Find the mean, median, and mode using the following data:

Exercise #1

12, 24, 23, 18, 31, 35, 10, 28, 29, 22, 36, 29, 32, 41, 27, 25

Exercise #2

72, 56, 39, 47, 52, 59, 35, 28, 14, 66, 55, 40, 38, 28, 55, 29

Exercise #3

114, 98, 81, 141, 92, 87, 103, 89, 100, 119, 85, 98, 105, 79. 91

Chapter Two

Create an Absolute, Relative, Cumulative, and Cumulative Relative Frequency Distribution using the following data:

Exercise #1

Reported Offense	Absolute Frequency
Assault without Weapon	298
Assault with Weapon	46
Domestic Violence	51
Theft	729
Public Disturbance	68
Alcohol/Drug	144
Traffic	1,813
Calls for Service	765
Miscellaneous	389
Total (N)	3,885

Exercise #2

Reported Offense	Absolute Frequency
Assault without Weapon	172
Assault with Weapon	54
Domestic Violence	68
Theft	523
Public Disturbance	55
Alcohol/Drug	159
Traffic	2,023
Calls for Service	3079
Miscellaneous	547
Total (N)	3,885

Chapter Three

Find the range, the variance, and the standard deviation of the following data:

Exercise #1

16, 62, 35, 23, 19, 53, 26, 63, 51, 28, 37, 42, 47, 29, 38, 41, 61

Exercise #2

37, 49, 72, 74, 16 26, 63, 54, 48, 34, 49, 51, 53, 68, 66, 35, 51

Exercise #3

175, 152, 223, 181, 201, 199, 176, 159, 164, 187, 169, 155, 219, 161, 213

Find the z scores for the following officers and designate which officer is the best performer based upon the issuing of citations across the three shifts. Also, find the shift mean and the standard deviation.

Exercise #4

	Employee	Production	Shift Mean	SD	Z Score
Day Shift					
	Robert	72			
	Allen	74			
	Betty	65			
	Jim	70			
Evening Shift					
	Sandra	74			
	William	67			
	Joan	73			
	Ed	65			
Night Shift					
	Rhonda	44			
	Rodney	52			
	Marcia	51			
	Steven	47			

Exercise #5

	Employee	Production	Shift Mean	SD	Z Score
Day Shift					
	Samuel	57			
	Patricia	74			
	Susan	62			
	Rodney	66			
Evening Shift					
	Jessie	78			
	Frank	62			
	Leroy	74			
	Jean	59			
Night Shift					
	Heather	49			
	Kara	57			
	Megan	55			
	Steven	42			

Note: There are no exercises for Chapter 4.

Chapter Five

Exercise #1

There is a question as to whether persons assigned to police precincts were selected based upon their gender. Perform a chi-square test and determine if there is a statistically significant difference in precinct assignment based upon gender.

	Male	Female
Precinct One	52	46
Precinct Two	64	62
Precinct Three	47	51

As the Chief, you have had a complaint brought to your attention that your officers are issuing verbal warnings, written warning, or issuing citations based upon the race of the driver. You have collected information on the actions of the officers from last month and have decided to run a Chi-Square test to see if the accusation may require further investigation or training.

Exercise #2

	Minority Drivers	White Drivers
Verbal Warning	52	46
Written Warning	64	62
Citation Issued	47	51

Chapter Six

Exercise #1

Covariation is found within our computation for correlation. Find and interpret Pearson's Product-Moment Correlation (r) for the height (shown in inches) and weight (shown in pounds) of the sample of officers as indicated in the following data:

Officer	Height	Weight
1	68	165
2	72	183
3	67	170
4	75	205
5	78	225
6	69	185
7	70	195
8	65	155

Exercise #2

Find and interpret Pearson's Product-Moment Correlation (r) for the weight (in pounds) and fuel mileage (in gallons) of the following vehicles in your fleet of patrol cars:

Vehicle #	Weight	M.P.G.
1	3,456	23
2	3,162	26
3	3,621	22
4	3,173	26
5	3,850	20
6	3,350	25

Chapter Seven

Exercise

In simple regression we are going to take the same information as above, add a little more data, and then run our simple regression. In simple regression we are using only one predictor variable (height) to predict what will happen to our dependent variable (weight).

Officer	Height	Weight
1	68	165
2	72	183
3	67	170
4	75	205
5	78	225
6	69	185
7	70	195
8	65	155
9	66	157
10	73	195
11	77	235
12	65	145

Run the regression and then interpret the results with respect to how well height would serve to predict weight. If a person were 67 inches tall (5' 7") how tall would be predict they would be if they came from the same population from which this sample was drawn? What would that prediction be if we wanted to be 95% confident that the person would fall within our predicted range of weight?

Chapter Eight

Exercise

In multiple regression we are doing the same thing we did in simple regression but we are adding more predictor variables to improve the accuracy of our prediction. Run a multiple regression using Excel (do this just like simple regression except capture all of the X columns at the same time when you tell the program where the data is). Run the regression and predict the height of someone who is 6' 2" (74") with a waist size of 38 inches, with a confidence of 95%.

Officer	Height (inches)	Waist (inches)	Weight (pounds)
1	72	35	198
2	75	37	220
3	68	34	180
4	65	31	155
5	70	35	175
6	70	35	180
7	71	36	190
8	69	35	175
9	68	32	160
10	63	29	145
11	77	38	250
12	75	39	235

Chapter Nine

Exercise

In this chapter we have learned how to use the t test to check for a significant difference between the means of two sets of data. While we could test using a one-tailed test if we were able to anticipate a direction of movement, we are always safe to run the two-tailed test. And, as the two-tailed test takes a higher level of difference to declare a significant finding I always use the two-tailed test.

In Chapter Nine we spent our time looking at how the t test worked and the mechanics of performing the test by hand. However, we can us Excel to perform the test for us. We use the same procedure in setting up our problem in Excel as before, but this time when the program asks us to select the test we want to run we will select t Test: Two-Sample Assuming Equal Variables.

For our test we will make up some test scores taken from two sets of officers. One set will be of officers with more than ten years of experience in law enforcement and the other set will be officers with less than five years of experience in law enforcement. We will run the test at the default of an alpha of 0.05.

Test Scores	
<5	>10
88	94
92	96
75	82
69	78
77	86
83	87
85	92
92	93
89	97
90	94
95	98

Chapter Ten

Exercise

To practice our ANOVA we will use the example from Chapter Ten in our text, but I am going to change the numbers on you. Enter the data into your Excel spreadsheet, go to Data Analysis, select ANOVA, and have fun. Of course, as in our example in the actual chapter we are looking for a significant difference in test scores among the three groups of students based upon our three different methods of instruction.

Score of Test Groups of Students

(S-1)	(S-2)	(S-3)
92	90	96
89	87	94
85	85	96
90	87	94
91	90	97
92	89	95
79	81	88
84	80	89
83	89	93

Chapter Exercise Solutions

Chapter One

Exercise #1
Mean = 26.375 (26 rounded); Median = 27.5; Mode = 29

Exercise #2
Mean = 44.562 (45 rounded); Median = 43.5; Mode = 28

Exercise #3
Mean = 98.8 (99 rounded); Median = 98; Mode = 98

Mean	98.8
Standard Error	4.209060522
Median	98
Mode	98
Standard Deviatior	16.3016213
Sample Variance	265.7428571
Kurtosis	2.01610384
Skewness	1.290195559
Range	62
Minimum	79
Maximum	141
Sum	1482
Count	15

Chapter Two

Exercise #1

Category	Ab. Fre.	Rel. Fre. (%)	Cum. Fre.	Cum. Rel. (%)
Assault w/o Weapon	298	7	298	7
Assault with Weapon	46	1	344	8
Domestic Violence	51	1	395	9
Theft	729	17	1,124	26
Public Disturbance	68	2	1,192	28
Alcohol/Drug	144	3	1,336	31
Traffic	1,813	42	3,149	73
Calls for Service	765	18	3,914	91
Miscellaneous	389	9	4,303	100
Total (N)	4,303	100		

Exercise #2

Category	Ab. Fre.	Rel. Fre. %	Cum. Fre.	Cum.Rel. %	
Assault without Weapon	172	3	172	3	
Assault with Weapon	54	1	226	4	
Domestic Violence	68	1	294	5	
Theft	523	8	817	13	
Public Disturbance	55	1	872	14	
Alcohol/Drug	159	2	1031	16	
Traffic	2023	30	3054	46	
Calls for Service	3079	46	6133	92	
Miscellaneous	547	8	6680	100%	
Total (N)	6680	100%			

Chapter Three

Exercise #1

Range = 47; Variance = 224.8897059 (224.9 rounded); Standard Deviation = 14.99632308 (15 rounded)

Exercise #2

Range = 58; Variance = 263.9411765 (264 rounded); Standard Deviation = 16.24626654 (16.3 rounded)

Exercise #3

Column1	
Mean	182.2666667
Standard Error	6.119030943
Median	176
Mode	#N/A
Standard Deviation	23.69890494
Sample Variance	561.6380952
Kurtosis	-1.085336814
Skewness	0.484660877
Range	71
Minimum	152
Maximum	223
Sum	2734
Count	15

Z-score Exercise #4

	Employee	Production	Shift Mean	SD	Z-Score
Day Shift					
	Robert	72	73.75	3.78	−0.46
	Allen	74			0.07
	Betty	65			−2.32
	Jim	70			−0.99
Evening Shift					
	Sandra	74	70.00	4.69	0.85
	William	67			−0.64
	Joan	73			0.64
	Ed	65			−1.07
Night Shift					
	Rhonda	44	45.50	3.12	−0.48
	Rodney	52			2.08
	Marcia	51			1.76
	Steven	47			0.48

At a z score of 2.08, Rodney is the top producer if we are measuring production by the issuing of citations. The shift means and standard deviations are as shown above.

Z-score Exercise #5

At a z-score of 1.29, Patricia is the top producer across all three shifts. Conversely, at −1.0 Heather is the least productive member of the three shifts. In z-scores we are measuring the distance from the mean to the individual z-score on the positive or negative side of the mean.

Employee	Production	Shift Mean	SD	Z-Score
Day Shift				
Samuel	57	64.75	7.18	1.00
Patricia	74			1.29
Susan	62			0.04
Rodney	66			0.73
Evening Shift				
Jessie	78	68.25	9.18	0.63
Frank	62			−0.14
Leroy	74			0.52
Jean	59			−0.35
Night Shift				
Heather	49	50.75	6.75	−1.0
Kara	57			0.19
Megan	55			0.04
Steven	42			−0.56

Note: There are no exercises for Chapter 4.

Chapter Five

Exercise #1

	Male	Female	Marginal
Precinct One	52(50)	46(48)	98
Precinct Two	64(64)	62(62)	126
Precinct Three	47(50)	51(48)	98
Marginal	163	159	322

$$0.08 + 0.08 + 0.0 + 0.0 + 0.12 + 0.19 = 0.47$$
$$df = (3 - 1)(2 - 1) = 2$$
Table Chi-Square = 5.991 at alpha = 0.05

Computed Chi-Square at 0.47 is not a significant finding, and we would fail to reject the null hypothesis. There does not appear to be a significant difference in assignment to the precincts based upon gender.

Exercise #2

	Minority Drivers	White Drivers	Marginal
Verbal Warning	52(50)	46(48)	98
Written Warning	64(64)	62(62)	126
Citation Issued	47(50)	51(48)	98
Marginal	163	159	322

$$0.08 + 0.08 + 0.0 + 0.0 + 0.18 + 0.19 = 0.53$$
$$df = (3 - 1)(2 - 1) = 2$$
Table Chi-Square = 5.991 at alpha = 0.05

Chapter Six

Exercise #1

	Height	*Weight*
Height	1	
Weight	0.945761	1

The correlation between the height and weight of the officers is 0.94, which is a very high correlation and would tell us that we could use height to predict the weight of the population that this sample of officers was drawn from. If we square the correlation we have 0.8944638, or rounded to 0.90, and this tells us that 90% of the question of weight is answered by the height of the individual if we only use one predictor (height).

The r of 1 that is seen running at a diagonal from upper left to lower right is the variable (height and weight) being compared to itself, thus a perfect correlation of 1.

Exercise #2

	Weight	*MPG*
Weight	1	
MPG	-0.99021	1

Chapter Seven

Simple Regression, Exercise #1

Regression Statistics	
Multiple R	0.958044742
R Square	0.917849727
Adjusted R Sq	0.9096347
Standard Error	8.410642971
Observations	12

ANOVA

	df	SS	MS	F	Significance F
Regression	1	7903.527515	7903.527515	111.7281414	9.54046E-07
Residual	10	707.3891518	70.73891518		
Total	11	8610.916667			

	Coefficients	Standard Error	t Stat	P-value	Lower 95%
Intercept	-229.1754641	39.21929303	-5.843436901	0.000163052	-316.5614947
Height	5.87586458	0.555892086	10.57015333	9.54046E-07	4.637259826

As we look at our Excel output, we see that the adjusted R is 0.9096347, which rounds to 0.91 and converts to 91%. In other words, 91% of the question of weight is answered by height in our sample, which we could then generalize to the population from which the sample was drawn.

If we look at the F and compare it to the Significance of F, we see that F is very much larger than the Significance F and that this is a good regression model to use if we are only using one predictor variable.

If we next look at the lower part of our printout, we see that the coefficient for height is 5.876 (rounded) and that our intercept is −229.176 (rounded). The P-values are also very good as they are both very significant. To predict the weight of someone who was 67" tall (5'7") we would take the height of the person we were trying to predict the weight of and multiply that height in inches by the coefficient for height, and then subtract the intercept (we are subtracting because there is a minus sign (−) in front of the intercept coefficient). When we do this, we come up with:

$$Y = 67(5.876) - 229.176$$
$$Y = 393.692 - 229.176$$
$$Y = 164.516 \text{ pounds}$$

We could round this to 165 pounds, but if we wanted to be 95% sure that our prediction would be correct we would take the standard error from out printout (8.411 rounded) and we would take that standard error and multiply it by 1.95, which is the z score for two standard deviations (which covers 95% of the data).

$$66 + 8.411(1.95) = 166 + 16.40 = 184.4$$
$$166 - 8.411(1.95) = 166 - 16.40 = 149.6$$

If we rounded out numbers we would predict, with 95% confidence, that someone who was 5'7" tall would weigh between 150 and 184 pounds.

Chapter Eight

Multiple Regression, Exercise #1

Regression Statistics					
Multiple R	0.962442195				
R Square	0.926294978				
Adjusted R Sq	0.909916084				
Standard Error	9.647402827				
Observations	12				

ANOVA					
	df	SS	MS	F	Significance F
Regression	2	10527.26523	5263.632617	56.55418442	8.01192E-06
Residual	9	837.6514318	93.07238131		
Total	11	11364.91667			

	Coefficients	Standard Error	t Stat	P-value	Lower 95%
Intercept	-340.056135	61.88781357	-5.494718837	0.000382794	-480.0560958
Height	7.545799355	2.191119073	3.443810722	0.00734616	2.58914365
Waist	-0.041911625	3.140438517	-0.013345788	0.989643079	-7.146077111

As we look at our Excel printout and view the Adjusted R, we notice that we have a value of 0.909916084, which we can round to 0.91. Moving the decimal two places to the right we have 91% which tells us that our model using height and waist size is accounting for 91% of the question of what a person from the population from which the sample was drawn is likely to weight.

We know from our exercise in simple regression that we need to take the coefficients of height and waist size and place them into our equation and then subtract the value of the intercept (we are subtracting because there is a minus sign (−) in front of the coefficient. We also know from looking at the F and the Significance F that we have a pretty darn good multiple regression to use to predict the weight of our subject. We would put our numbers together like this (as you can see, I am rounding some of the numbers):

$$Y = 74(7.55) + 38(-0.04) - 340.1$$
$$Y = 558.7 + (-1.5) - 340.1$$
$$Y = 217.1 \text{ pounds}$$

As we did before, if we want to be 95% confident in what we are predicting, we would multiple the standard error (9.65 rounded) by 1.95 and then add and subtract that amount from our central prediction of 217 pounds (rounded).

$$217 + 9.65(1.95) = 217 + 18.8 = 235.8$$
$$217 - 9.65(1.95) = 217 - 18.8 = 198.2$$

If we rounded out numbers we would predict, with 95% confidence, that someone who was 6'2" tall and had a waist size of 38" would weigh between 198 and 236 pounds.

Chapter Nine

t-Test Assuming Equal Variance, Exercise #1

	<5	>10
Mean	85	90.63636364
Variance	67.2	42.25454545
Observations	11	11
Pooled Variance	54.72727273	
Hypothesized Mean Difference	0	
df	20	
t Stat	−1.786810295	
P(T<=t) one-tail	0.044568059	
t Critical one-tail	1.724718243	
P(T<=t) two-tail	0.089136117	
t Critical two-tail	2.085963447	

In this exercise, we are interested in testing for a significant difference between two sets of test scores, one set from officers with less than five years of experience and one set from officers with more than ten years of experience. We are using a t test assuming equal variances as we always assume there are equal variances unless we have a reason to think otherwise.

As we look at our Excel printout, we see that the t Stat is −1.787 (rounded) and that the t Critical two-tailed is 2.086 (rounded). As our t Stat is smaller than our t Critical, we would fail to reject our null hypothesis that there is no significant difference between the test scores. Thus, it appears that the years of experience in law enforcement do not make a significant difference in how well the officers score on this particular test. We can also look at the P for a two-tailed test (0.09 rounded) and this tells us the same thing, as the P is larger than 0.05, and we would need a P of 0.05 or lower to claim significance.

Chapter Ten

ANOVA, Single Factor, Exercise #1

Anova: Single Factor							
SUMMARY							
Groups	Count	Sum		Average	Variance		
(S-1)	9	785		87.22222222	21.44444444		
(S-2)	9	778		86.44444444	14.02777778		
(S-3)	9	842		93.55555556	9.777777778		
ANOVA							
urce of Variati	SS	df		MS	F	P-value	F crit
Between Grou	273.8518519	2		136.9259259	9.07796194	0.001159395	3.402826105
Within Groups	362	24		15.08333333			
Total	635.8518519	26					

Our purpose in running this test is to try to determine whether or not one method of instruction is better than another when it comes to student outcomes on the final exam at the end of the term. If we look at the average test scores at the top of our printout, we can easily see that the S-3 group of students, who were taught using a text and lectures, overall scored much better than the other two student groups. If we look down to the F and the F crit, we can also see that the F is much higher than the F crit, and this tells us that we do have a significant difference in our testing outcomes based upon instructional method. We can also look at the P-value, which confirms our comparison of the F and F crit as the P-value is well below 0.05 and indicates we do have a very significant finding in our test. By the way, remember that anytime we see the letter E in a P-value we automatically know we have a significant finding in our test.

Tables and Charts

Areas Beneath the Normal Curve

Z	.00	.01	.02	.03	.04	.05	.06	.07	.08	.09
.0	.0000	.0040	.0080	.0120	.0160	.0199	.0239	.0279	.0319	.0359
.1	.0398	.0438	.0478	.0517	.0557	.0596	.0636	.0675	.0714	.0753
.2	.0793	.0832	.0871	.0910	.0948	.0987	.1026	.1064	.1103	.1141
.3	.1179	.1217	.1255	.1293	.1331	.1368	.1406	.1443	.1480	.1517
.4	.1554	.1591	.1628	.1664	.1700	.1736	.1772	.1808	.1844	.1879
.5	.1915	.1950	.1985	.2019	.2054	.2088	.2123	.2157	.2190	.2224
.6	.2257	.2291	.2324	.2357	.2389	.2422	.2454	.2486	.2518	.2549
.7	.2580	.2612	.2642	.2673	.2704	.2734	.2764	.2794	.2823	.2852
.8	.2881	.2910	.2939	.2967	.2995	.3023	.3051	.3078	.3106	.3133
.9	.3159	.3186	.3212	.3238	.3264	.3289	.3315	.3340	.3365	.3389
1.0	.3413	.3438	.3461	.3485	.3508	.3531	.3554	.3577	.3599	.3621
1.1	.3643	.3665	.3686	.3708	.3729	.3749	.3770	.3790	.3810	.3830
1.2	.3849	.3869	.3888	.3907	.3925	.3944	.3962	.3980	.3997	.4015
1.3	.4032	.4049	.4066	.4082	.4099	.4115	.4131	.4147	.4162	.4177
1.4	.4192	.4207	.4222	.4236	.4251	.4265	.4279	.4292	.4306	.4319
1.5	.4332	.4345	.4357	.4370	.4382	.4394	.4406	.4418	.4429	.4441

Z	.00	.01	.02	.03	.04	.05	.06	.07	.08	.09
1.6	.4452	.4463	.4474	.4484	.4495	.4505	.4515	.4525	.4535	.4545
1.7	.4554	.4564	.4573	.4582	.4591	.4599	.4608	.4616	.4625	.4633
1.8	.4641	.4649	.4656	.4664	.4671	.4678	.4686	.4693	.4699	.4706
1.9	.4713	.4719	.4726	.4732	.4738	.4744	.4750	.4756	.4761	.4767
2.0	.4772	.4778	.4783	.4788	.4793	.4798	.4803	.4808	.4812	.4817
2.1	.4821	.4826	.4830	.4834	.4838	.4842	.4846	.4850	.4854	.4857
2.2	.4861	.4864	.4868	.4871	.4875	.4878	.4881	.4884	.4887	.4890
2.3	.4893	.4896	.4898	.4901	.4904	.4906	.4909	.4911	.4913	.4916
2.4	.4918	.4920	.4922	.4925	.4927	.4929	.4931	.4932	.4934	.4936
2.5	.4938	.4940	.4941	.4943	.4945	.4946	.4948	.4949	.4951	.4942
2.6	.4953	.4955	.4956	.4957	.4959	.4960	.4961	.4962	.4963	.4964
2.7	.4965	.4966	.4967	.4968	.4969	.4970	.4971	.4972	.4973	.4974
2.8	.4974	.4975	.4976	.4977	.4977	.4978	.4979	.4979	.4980	.4981
2.9	.4981	.4982	.4982	.4983	.4984	.4984	.4985	.4985	.4986	.4986
3.0	.4986	.4987	.4987	.4988	.4988	.4989	.4989	.4989	.4990	.4990

t Values Needed for Rejection of the Null Hypothesis

df	One-Tailed Test			Two-Tailed Test		
	0.10	0.05	0.01	0.10	0.05	0.01
1	3.078	6.314	31.821	6.314	12.706	63.657
2	1.886	2.92	6.965	2.92	4.303	9.925
3	1.638	2.353	4.541	2.353	3.182	5.841
4	1.533	2.132	3.747	2.132	2.776	4.604
5	1.476	2.015	3.365	2.015	2.571	4.032
6	1.440	1.943	3.143	1.943	2.447	3.708
7	1.415	1.895	2.998	1.895	2.365	3.5
8	1.397	1.86	2.897	1.86	2.306	3.356
9	1.383	1.833	2.822	1.833	2.262	3.25
10	1.372	1.813	2.764	1.813	2.228	3.17
11	1.364	1.796	2.718	1.796	2.201	3.106
12	1.356	1.783	2.681	1.783	2.179	3.055
13	1.35	1.771	2.651	1.771	2.161	3.013
14	1.345	1.762	2.625	1.762	2.145	2.977
15	1.341	1.753	2.603	1.753	2.132	2.947
16	1.337	1.746	2.584	1.746	2.12	2.921
17	1.334	1.74	2.567	1.74	2.11	2.898
18	1.331	1.734	2.553	1.734	2.101	2.879
19	1.328	1.729	2.54	1.729	2.093	2.861
20	1.326	1.725	2.528	1.725	2.086	2.846
21	1.323	1.721	2.518	1.721	2.08	2.832

	One-Tailed Test				Two-Tailed Test		
df	0.10	0.05	0.01	df	0.10	0.05	0.01
22	1.321	1.717	2.509	22	1.717	2.074	2.819
23	1.32	1.714	2.5	23	1.714	2.069	2.808
24	1.318	1.711	2.492	24	1.711	2.064	2.797
25	1.317	1.708	2.485	25	1.708	2.06	2.788
26	1.315	1.706	2.479	26	1.706	2.056	2.779
27	1.314	1.704	2.473	27	1.704	2.052	2.771
28	1.313	1.701	2.467	28	1.701	2.049	2.764
29	1.312	1.699	2.462	29	1.699	2.045	2.757
30	1.311	1.698	2.458	30	1.698	2.043	2.75
35	1.306	1.69	2.438	35	1.69	2.03	2.724
40	1.303	1.684	2.424	40	1.684	2.021	2.705
45	1.301	1.68	2.412	45	1.68	2.014	2.69
50	1.299	1.676	2.404	50	1.676	2.009	2.678
55	1.297	1.673	2.396	55	1.673	2.004	2.668
60	1.296	1.671	2.39	60	1.671	2.001	2.661
65	1.295	1.669	2.385	65	1.669	1.997	2.654
70	1.294	1.667	2.381	70	1.667	1.995	2.648
75	1.293	1.666	2.377	75	1.666	1.992	2.643
80	1.292	1.664	2.374	80	1.664	1.99	2.639
85	1.292	1.663	2.371	85	1.663	1.989	2.635
90	1.291	1.662	2.369	90	1.662	1.987	2.632

	One-Tailed Test				Two-Tailed Test		
df	0.10	0.05	0.01	df	0.10	0.05	0.01
95	1.291	1.661	2.366	95	1.661	1.986	2.629
100	1.29	1.66	2.364	100	1.66	1.984	2.626
Infinity	1.282	1.645	2.327	Infinity	1.645	1.96	2.576

Critical Values for Analysis of Variance or F Test

df for the Denominator	Type I Error Rate	df for the Numerator					
		1	2	3	4	5	6
1	.01	4052.00	4999.00	5403.00	5625.00	5764.00	5859.00
	.05	162.00	200.00	216.00	225.00	230.00	234.00
	.10	39.90	49.50	53.60	55.80	57.20	58.20
2	.01	98.50	99.00	99.17	99.25	99.30	99.33
	.05	18.51	19.00	19.17	19.25	19.30	19.33
	.10	8.53	9.00	9.16	9.24	9.29	9.33
3	.01	34.12	30.82	29.46	28.71	28.24	27.91
	.05	10.13	9.55	9.28	9.12	9.01	8.94
	.10	5.54	5.46	5.39	5.34	5.31	5.28
4	.01	21.20	18.00	16.70	15.98	15.52	15.21
	.05	7.71	6.95	6.59	6.39	6.26	6.16
	.10	.55	4.33	4.19	4.11	4.05	4.01
5	.01	16.26	13.27	12.06	11.39	10.97	10.67
	.05	6.61	5.79	5.41	5.19	5.05	4.95
	.10	4.06	3.78	3.62	3.52	3.45	3.41
6	.01	13.75	10.93	9.78	9.15	8.75	8.47
	.05	5.99	5.14	4.76	4.53	4.39	4.28
	.10	3.78	3.46	3.29	3.18	3.11	3.06
7	.01	12.25	9.55	8.45	7.85	7.46	7.19
	.05	5.59	4.74	4.35	4.12	3.97	3.87
	.10	3.59	3.26	3.08	2.96	2.88	2.83
8	.01	11.26	8.65	7.59	7.01	6.63	6.37
	.05	5.32	4.46	4.07	3.84	3.69	3.58
	.10	3.46	3.11	2.92	2.81	2.73	2.67

df for the Denominator	Type I Error Rate	df for the Numerator					
		1	2	3	4	5	6
9	.01	10.56	8.02	6.99	6.42	6.06	5.80
	.05	5.12	4.26	3.86	3.63	3.48	3.37
	.10	3.36	3.01	2.81	2.69	2.61	2.55
10	.01	10.05	7.56	6.55	6.00	5.64	5.39
	.05	4.97	4.10	3.71	3.48	3.33	3.22
	.10	3.29	2.93	2.73	2.61	2.52	2.46
11	.01	9.65	7.21	6.22	5.67	5.32	5.07
	.05	4.85	3.98	3.59	3.36	3.20	3.10
	.10	3.23	2.86	2.66	2.54	2.45	2.39
12	.01	9.33	6.93	5.95	5.41	5.07	4.82
	.05	4.75	3.89	3.49	3.26	3.11	3.00
	.10	3.18	2.81	2.61	2.48	2.40	2.33
13	.01	9.07	6.70	5.74	5.21	4.86	4.62
	.05	4 .67	3.81	3.41	3.18	3.03	2.92
	.10	3.14	2.76	2.56	2.43	2.35	2.28
14	.01	8.86	6.52	5.56	5.04	4.70	4.46
	.05	4.60	3.74	3.34	3.11	2.96	2.85
	.10	3.10	2.73	2.52	2.40	2.31	2.24
15	.01	8.68	6.36	5.42	4.89	4 .56	4.32
	.05	4.54	3.68	3.29	3.06	2.90	2.79
	.10	3.07	2.70	2.49	2.36	2.27	2.21
16	.01	8.53	6.23	5.29	4.77	4.44	4.20
	.05	4.49	3.63	3.24	3.01	2.85	2.74
	.10	3.05	2.67	2.46	2.33	2.24	2.18
17	.01	8.40	6.11	5.19	4.67	4.34	4.10
	.05	4.45	3.59	3.20	2 .97	2.81	2.70
	.10	3.03	2.65	2.44	2.31	2.22	2.15

df for the Denominator	Type I Error Rate	df for the Numerator					
		1	2	3	4	5	6
18	.01	8.29	6.01	5.09	4.58	4 .25	4.02
	.05	4.41	3.56	3.16	2.93	2.77	2.66
	.10	3.01	2.62	2.42	2.29	2.20	2.13
19	.01	8.19	5.93	5.01	4.50	4.17	3.94
	.05	4.38	3.52	3.13	2.90	2.74	2.63
	.10	2.99	2.61	2.40	2.27	2.18	2.11
20	.01	8.10	5.85	4.94	4.43	4.10	3.87
	.05	4.35	3.49	3.10	2.87	2.71	2.60
	.10	2.98	2.59	2.38	2.25	2.16	2.09
21	.01	8.02	5.78	4 .88	4.37	4.04	3.81
	.05	4.33	3.47	3.07	2.84	2.69	2.57
	.10	2.96	2.58	2.37	2.23	2.14	2.08
22	.01	7.95	5.72	4.82	4.31	3.99	3.76
	.05	4.30	3.44	3.05	2.82	2.66	2.55
	.10	2.95	2.56	2.35	2.22	2.13	2.06
23	.01	7.88	5.66	4 .77	4.26	3.94	3.71
	.05	4.28	3.42	3.03	2.80	2.64	2.53
	.10	2.94	2.55	2.34	2.21	2.12	2.05
24	.01	7.82	5.61	4.72	4.22	3.90	3.67
	.05	4.26	3.40	3.01	2.78	2.62	2.51
	.10	2.93	2.54	2.33	2.20	2.10	2.04
25	.01	7.77	5.57	4 .68	4.18	3.86	3.63
	.05	4.24	3.39	2.99	2.76	2.60	2.49
	.10	2.92	2.53	2.32	2.19	2.09	2.03
26	.01	7.72	5.53	4.64	4.14	3.82	3.59
	.05	4.23	3.37	2.98	2.74	2.59	2.48
	.10	2.91	2.52	2.31	2.18	2.08	2.01

df for the Denomi-nator	Type I Error Rate	df for the Numerator					
		1	2	3	4	5	6
27	.01	7.68	5.49	4.60	4.11	3.79	3.56
	.05	4.21	3.36	2.96	2.73	2.57	2.46
	.10	2.90	2.51	2.30	2.17	2.07	2.01
28	.01	7.64	5.45	4.57	4.08	3.75	3.53
	.05	4.20	3.34	2.95	2.72	2.56	2.45
	.10	2.89	2.50	2.29	2.16	2.07	2.00
29	.01	7.60	5.42	4.54	4.05	3.73	3.50
	.05	4.18	3.33	2.94	2.70	2.55	2.43
	.10	2.89	2.50	2.28	2.15	2.06	1.99
30	.01	7.56	5.39	4.51	4.02	3.70	3.47
	.05	4.17	3.32	2.92	2.69	2.53	2.42
	.10	2.88	2.49	2.28	2.14	2.05	1.98
35	.01	7.42	5.27	4.40	3.91	3.59	3.37
	.05	4.12	3.27	2.88	2.64	2.49	2.37
	.10	2.86	2.46	2.25	2.14	2 .02	1.95
40	.01	7.32	5.18	4.31	3.91	3.51	3.29
	.05	4.09	3.23	2.84	2.64	2.45	2.34
	.10	2.84	2.44	2.23	2.11	2.00	1.93
45	.01	7.23	5.11	4.25	3.83	3.46	3.23
	.05	4.06	3.21	2.81	2.61	2.42	2.31
	.10	2.82	2.43	2 .21	2.09	1.98	1.91
50	.01	7.17	5.06	4.20	3.77	3.41	3.19
	.05	4.04	3.18	2 .79	2.58	2.40	2.29
	.10	2.81	2.41	2.20	2.08	1.97	1.90
55	.01	7.12	5.01	4.16	3.72	3.37	3.15
	.05	4.02	3.17	2.77	2.56	2.38	2.27
	.10	2.80	2.40	2.19	2.06	1.96	1.89

df for the Denomi-nator	Type I Error Rate	df for the Numerator					
		1	2	3	4	5	6
60	.01	7.08	4.98	4.13	3.68	3.34	3.12
	.05	4.00	3.15	2.76	2.54	2.37	2.26
	.10	2.79	2.39	2.18	2.05	1.95	1.88
65	.01	7.04	4.95	4.10	3.65	3.31	3.09
	.05	3.99	3.14	2.75	2.53	2.36	2.24
	.10	2.79	2.39	2.17	2.04	1.94	1.87
70	.01	7.01	4.92	4.08	3.62	3.29	3.07
	.05	3.98	3.13	2.74	2.51	2.35	2.23
	.10	2.78	2.38	2 .16	2.03	1.93	1.86
75	.01	6.99	4.90	4.06	3.60	3.27	3.05
	.05	3.97	3.12	2.73	2.50	2.34	2.22
	.10	2.77	2.38	2.16	2.03	1.93	1.86
80	.01	3.96	4 .88	4.04	3.56	3.26	3.04
	.05	6.96	3.11	2.72	2.49	2.33	2.22
	.10	2.77	2.37	2.15	2.02	1.92	1.85
85	.01	6.94	4.86	4.02	3.55	3.24	3.02
	.05	3.95	3.10	2.71	2.48	2.32	2.21
	.10	2.77	2.37	2.15	2.01	1.92	1.85
90	.01	6.93	4.85	4.02	3.54	3.23	3.01
	.05	3.95	3.10	2.71	2.47	2.32	2.20
	.10	2.76	2.36	2.15	2.01	1.91	1.84
95	.01	6.91	4.84	4.00	3.52	3.22	3.00
	.05	3.94	3.09	2.70	2.47	2.31	2.20
	.10	2.76	2.36	2.14	2.01	1.91	1.84

df for the Denominator	*Type I Error Rate*			*df for the Numerator*			
		1	*2*	*3*	*4*	*5*	*6*
100	.01	6.90	4.82	3.98	3.51	3.21	2.99
	.05	3.94	3.09	2.70	2.46	2.31	2.19
	.10	2.76	2.36	2.14	2.00	1.91	1.83
Infinity	.01	6.64	4.61	3.78	3.32	3.02	2.80
	.05	3.84	3.00	2.61	2.37	2.22	2.10
	.10	2.71	2.30	2.08	1.95	1.85	1.78

Values of the Correlation Coefficient Needed for Rejection of the Null Hypothesis

	One-Tailed Test			Two-Tailed Test	
df	.05	.01	df	.05	.01
1	.9877	.9995	1	.9969	.9999
2	.9000	.9800	2	.9500	.9900
3	.8054	.9343	3	.8783	.9587
4	.7293	.8822	4	.8114	.9172
5	.6694	.8320	5	.7545	.8745
6	.6215	.7887	6	.7067	.8343
7	.5822	.7498	7	.6664	.7977
8	.5494	.7155	8	.6319	.7646
9	.5214	.6851	9	.6021	.7348
10	.4973	.6581	10	.5760	.7079
11	.4762	.6339	11	.5529	.6835
12	.4575	.6120	12	.5324	.6614
13	.4409	.5923	13	.5139	.6411
14	.4259	.5742	14	.4973	.6226
15	.4120	.5577	15	.4821	.6055
16	.4000	.5425	16	.4683	.5897
17	.3887	.5285	17	.4555	.5751
18	.3783	.5155	18	.4438	.5614
19	.3687	.5034	19	.4329	.5487
20	.3598	.4921	20	.4227	.5368
25	.3233	.4451	25	.3809	.4869
30	.2960	.4093	30	.3494	.4487
35	.2746	.3810	35	.3246	.4182
40	.2573	.3578	40	.3044	.3932
45	.2428	.3384	45	.2875	.3721
50	.2306	.3218	50	.2732	.3541
60	.2108	.2948	60	.2500	.3248
70	.1954	.2737	70	.2319	.3017
80	.1829	.2565	80	.2172	.2830
90	.1726	.2422	90	.2050	.2673
100	.1638	.2301	100	.1946	.2540

Critical Values for the Chi-Square Test

	Level of Significance		
df	.10	.05	.01
1	2.71	3.84	6.64
2	4.00	5.99	9.21
3	6.25	7.82	11.34
4	7.78	9.49	13.28
5	9.24	11.07	15.09
6	10.64	12.59	16.81
7	12.02	14.07	18.48
8	13.36	15.51	20.09
9	14.68	16.92	21.67
10	16.99	18.31	23.21
11	17.28	19.68	24.72
12	18.65	21.03	26.22
13	19.81	22.36	27.69
14	21.06	23.68	29.14
15	22.31	25.00	30.58
16	23.54	26.30	32.00
17	24.77	27.60	33.41
18	25.99	28.87	34.80
19	27.20	30.14	36.19
20	28.41	31.41	37.57
21	29.62	32.67	38.93
22	30.81	33.92	40.29
23	32.01	35.17	41.64
24	33.20	36.42	42.98
25	34.38	37.65	44.81
26	35.56	38.88	45.64
27	36.74	40.11	46.96
28	37.92	41.34	48.28
29	39.09	42.56	49.59
30	40.26	43.77	50.89

Index